Philip T. Woku

Grand Ave. Church.

Kansas City, Mo.

THE HIGHWAY OF GOD

Books by Dr. Ralph W. Sockman

LIVE FOR TOMORROW

RECOVERIES IN RELIGION

PARADOXES OF JESUS

THE UNEMPLOYED CARPENTER

MORALS OF TOMORROW

MEN OF THE MYSTERIES

SUBURBS OF CHRISTIANITY

THE REVIVAL OF THE CONVENTUAL LIFE IN THE
CHURCH OF ENGLAND IN THE NINETEENTH
CENTURY (DOCTOR'S THESIS)

THE HIGHWAY OF GOD

By Ralph W. Sockman

<small>THE LYMAN BEECHER LECTURES</small>

THE MACMILLAN COMPANY · *New York*

1942

PRINTED IN THE UNITED STATES OF AMERICA
BY THE VAIL-BALLOU PRESS, INC., BINGHAMTON, N. Y.

*Dedicated
to the memory
of my son
William*

ACKNOWLEDGMENTS

To Dean Luther A. Weigle and the Divinity School Faculty of Yale University for the invitation to deliver the Lyman Beecher Lectures and for their characteristically gracious hospitality; to Dean Emeritus Charles Reynolds Brown for the inspiration of his sympathetic presence throughout the lectures; to the body of students for their encouraging and sustained support; to the alumni whose fellowship made the stay at Yale a period of spiritual refreshment; to Miss Harriet C. Woodworth, M.A. for valuable editorial aid; to the Reverend G. Paul Butler, Ph.D. for illuminating insights; to Mrs. Helen V. Putnam, Mrs. Helen Hiller Palmer and Miss Juliette Endly for their most cooperative secretarial assistance—to all these I am indebted beyond my power to repay.

GUIDEPOSTS TO THE HIGHWAY

The invitation to deliver the Lyman Beecher Lectures at Yale University is a signal honor which mingles apprehension with appreciation. The question at once rises in the mind of the recipient: Is there anything significant left to be said in a lectureship which for seventy years has explored the subject of preaching by its leading exponents?

The present lecturer's first impulse was to survey the work of his predecessors, with the thought that there may have been certain earlier emphases which now need revival. In the course of this study the thought occurred: Why not go still further back to the first Christian appraisal of preaching, that is, to Our Lord's own estimate of the great popular preacher of his day, John the Baptist. The occasion of that analysis is recorded by both Matthew (11:2–20) and Luke (7:19–35) in strikingly parallel language.

The messengers of John had come, asking "Art thou he that should come? Or look we for another?" After Jesus had sent them back with his message to the Baptist, he turned to the spectators and asked: "What went ye out into the wilderness for to see?" Inasmuch as John had applied to himself the words of Isaiah, "The voice of him that crieth in the wilderness," (Isaiah 40:3), it would seem appropriate and imperative to consider the wilderness setting in which the prophet's voice is raised now as then. Chapter I attempts a prophet's eye view of the confused scene, the region of lost landmarks, through which God's guide is to prepare the way of the Lord.

Then in answer to his own question, our Lord said: "A reed shaken by the wind?" The query lifts the issue of the preacher's relation to the currents of influence which play upon him. How far is the everlasting gospel affected by the time and place of its delivery? What is the relation of the eternal and the timely, of the absolute and the relative? That is the burden of the second chapter.

Then Jesus went on: "But what went ye out for to see? A prophet?" What is it to be a prophet of God? How can a preacher know when he is speaking the word of the Lord? What is inspiration and where are the sources of revelation? With these issues Chapter III essays to deal.

Listen to our Lord again: "A prophet? Yea, I say unto you, and much more than a prophet. This is he of whom it is written, 'Behold, I send my messenger before thy face, which shall prepare thy way before thee.'" What is it to be "more than a prophet"? How is the messenger to prepare the way for his message? In trying to follow the Lord, do we open a road for him to follow us? What is the cure of souls? Such is the line of thought pursued in Chapter IV.

Jesus then went on to utter a strange word: "I say unto you, among those that are born of women there is not a greater prophet than John the Baptist: but he that is least in the Kingdom of God is greater than he." What did John, the equal of the greatest prophets, lack? What is the secret of the Kingdom which he missed? Is the Kingdom to come here or only hereafter? Are we muting some old notes which are needed to give harmony to our modern life? Is there a force we forget? These are some of the questions faced in the fifth chapter.

Then Jesus turns his analysis from John to the crowd and says: "Whereunto then shall I liken the men of this generation? . . . They are like unto children sitting in the market place and calling one to another and saying, 'We have piped unto you, and ye have not danced; we have mourned to you and ye have not wept.' For John the Baptist came neither eating bread nor drinking wine; and ye say, 'He hath a devil.' The Son of man is come eating and drinking and ye say, 'Behold a glutton and a winebibber, a friend of publicans and sinners.' But wisdom is justified of all her children." Without pressing the analogy too far, we believe we can see our contemporary constituency mirrored in the crowd addressed by Jesus. During the 1920's we had a liberalism which called the piping tunes to which it asked the church to dance, and during the 1930's we have had a pessimism which calls the funeral dirges to which it still asks the church to weep. How are the children of wisdom to satisfy the children of the market place? Can we be realistic and yet be saved by hope? Such will be the theme of the last chapter.

In this preview it is apparent that I am not using this lectureship to specialize on any single phase of the ministerial office, or to explore deeply any philosophical or theological aspects of the preacher's message. My undertaking is more in the nature of an orientation course for the young ministers who have been called to the kingdom for a time like this, and we hope it may serve also as a reorientation course for those of us who are now bewildered by the encompassing confusion. I believe there is quite as much need today for a fresh map of our field as for deeper mines of information.

When a book finally is frozen into form by the publisher, the author is haunted by the afterthoughts of what should have been added to clarify and complete. There is only One, however, who is both "author and finisher of our faith." This volume aspires to give directions rather than definitions.

RALPH W. SOCKMAN

New York City,
November 1, 1941.

CONTENTS

CONTENTS

CHAPTER I

A VOICE IN THE WILDERNESS

The voice of one crying in the wilderness, Prepare ye
the way of the Lord, make his paths straight.

LUKE 3:4

> Arise, oh, prophet, watch and hearken
> And with my Will thy soul engird,
> Roam the grey seas, the roads that darken
> And burn men's hearts with this my Word.
> ALEXANDER PUSHKIN, *The Prophet*.

A VOICE IN THE WILDERNESS

1. *From Confidence to Confusion*

Lyman Beecher, in whose honor this lectureship was founded, expressed the optimistic outlook of his own ministry when he said, "I felt as if the conversion of the world to Christ was near." The present lecturer was called to continue this significant series at a time which entertains no such sunny confidence. The conversion of the world to Christ seems now "a far-off divine event" even to the most optimistic liberals, while so-called realists have repudiated the possibility of Christ's Kingdom ever coming in history.

If that hopefulness of yesterday is gone beyond recovery, it has not escaped beyond the borders of memory. Some of us recall the slogan of the Student Volunteer Movement thirty years ago: "The Evangelization of the World in This Generation." That expectation seemed justified in the light of missionary progress and zeal. The finest products of American, English, and Continental universities were enlisting in the Christian crusade with the result that the areas of heathendom on our missionary maps were shrinking like patches of snow before the spring sun. If the world was not about to be converted to Christ, at least it was about to be evangelized.

When the youth of my generation talked about "going overseas," the expression had not the sinister connotation of today. They had in mind the great missionary enter-

3

prise of the church, or perhaps the diplomatic and consular service of the government, or the foreign departments of expanding business. It was the Edwardian Era and the Victorian upholstery had not been stripped from the hard facts of life. Sir Edward Grey had not yet seen "the lights of Europe going out," as he said, on that fateful August morning of 1914. Europe was the "old world," and its age seemed to imply permanence. Britain was the seat of an Empire on whose shores the sun never set; Russia seemed frozen into static subservience to the "Little Father"; France was the land of happy peasants, gay Parisians and self-imposed American exiles; Italy was the mecca of the tourist with its holidays and holy places; Germany was the country to which our teachers went for graduate study, especially our professors of theology.

To be sure, there was a war now and then. For instance, Russia and Japan had gone to arms, but it seemed to us a kind of theatrical affair on a distant stage, rather a sporting proposition between cocky, little Japan and great, bearish Russia. It appeared too remote to raise any serious question of our becoming involved. Also, America had taken on a little war of her own at the turn of the century, but Admiral Dewey disposed of that with more ease than his namesake has enjoyed in cleaning up the rackets of New York City. The world of my student days seemed secure. As President Tucker of Dartmouth in his lectures on this Foundation had said some time before: "Christianity is in the blood of the races now in power." The world was controlled by "Christian nations." And if they had wars, at least they were regarded as good Christian wars.

The fact is that I do not recall hearing any sermons in my youth on the sin of war. There were some high school orations ending on the high note of Tennyson's "Parliament of Man, the Federation of the World." And pious hopes for world peace were sometimes expressed from the pulpit. But sins which the preachers of thirty and forty years ago attacked were drunkenness, lust, theft, and others of the personal repertoire. The international framework was taken for granted.

We were no doubt fortified in this optimism by the fact that we lived in "God's Country." That is what our fathers called this land of America. And there was little wonder. Ours was a land blessed with boundless resources and bounded by two protecting oceans. Immigrants were streaming into our ports in a ceaseless current, looking for the liberty and wealth which to Europeans were synonymous with the American way of life. Our money was as good as gold, for it was redeemable in gold. We worried about our private debts, but not about our national solvency. It was "God's Country." We were told on commencement occasions that we had to struggle to climb the ladder of fortune, but it was always confidently asserted that there was plenty of room at the top; and it would have been rank heresy to question whether the ladder was secure at the bottom.

The sunny confidence of that time was reflected in the following polished sentences of a popular preacher, Dr. Newell Dwight Hillis: "Laws are becoming more just; rulers more humane; music is becoming sweeter and books wiser; homes are happier and the individual heart is becoming at once more just and gentle. For today art, industry, invention, literature, learning and government, all these are captives marching in Christ's triumphant procession up the hill of fame." [1] Yes, America was "God's Country," and the world was evolving into God's Kingdom.

[1] Quoted by Mark Sullivan, *Our Times*, Vol. I, p. 364, Scribner's.

From that optimism of yesterday the pendulum has swung to a pessimism unprecedented in American thought. In Edna St. Vincent Millay's *Conversation at Midnight*, Ricardo exclaims:

Man has never been the same since God died.
He has taken it very hard. Why, you'd think it was only
    yesterday,
The way he takes it.
Not that he says much, but he laughs much louder than he
    used to,
And he can't bear to be left alone even for a minute, and he
    can't
Sit still.

.   .   .   .

He gets along pretty well as long as it's daylight: he works
    very hard
And he amuses himself very hard with the many cunning
    amusements
This clever age affords.
But it's all no use: the moment it begins to get dark, as soon
    as it's night
He goes out and howls over the grave of God.[2]

And in Millay's interpretation it is midnight in New York, midnight in Paris, midnight in London, midnight in Madrid.

Where the belief in God died, the loss led to another casualty. When Thomas Hardy failed to find divine support for his faith, he urged his contemporaries to face

life with dependence placed
On the human heart's resource alone,

[2] Edna St. Vincent Millay: *Conversation at Midnight*. Harper & Bros., 1937. Part IV, lines 11–16, 23–27.

In brotherhood bonded close and graced
With loving kindness fully blown,
And visioned help unsought, unknown.[3]

But "the brave new world" of the liberated humanists has turned out to be the burial ground of their social dreams. "Men in the nineteenth century were sad that they could no longer believe in God; they are more deeply saddened now by the fact that they can no longer believe in man." [4] Our generation has lost faith in the cleverness of the learned and the competence of the common man. In a day when democracy is the beloved shibboleth of liberal thought, we have a waning respect for man's social ability—a paradox to give us pause.

Paradoxically, too, the age which has glorified man's scientific achievements has pronounced the most humiliating verdict on the value of man himself. Somewhat silenced now are the mechanists who think of man as a "mere organic or inorganic complex." But vocal are the pessimists who have reduced man to the status of a moral pygmy devoid of dignity and destiny. Not only are values in danger, but the very principles by which we live are imperiled. The mood of the time is one of quiet desperation.

Faith in specific reforms has been widely undermined. Uprooted from our traditional certainties, our temper is that of spiritual refugees rather than of social explorers, venturing forth to pioneer new fields. Every human relation seems verging toward an alien environment. Powerful centrifugal forces pull everything toward the periphery of chaos. Institutions have developed a thousand inconsistencies. Schools, churches, courts, governments are floundering in a bog of bewilderment. Such is the wilderness

[3] Thomas Hardy: *A Plaint to Man.*
[4] Irwin Edman: *Candle in the Dark*, Viking Press, p. 10

wherein is to be heard the voice of one crying, "Prepare ye the way of the Lord."

Moreover, ours is a listening wilderness. Not only are bewildered men listening for voices, but many are in the state of near-hysteria wherein they are hearing voices. No Pied Piper from Berlin has yet gained any following worthy of note in America. However, demagogues rush in where dictators fear to tread. Cults capitalize on the uncertainty of the pulpit, and the more dogmatically they announce their bizarre beliefs, the stronger their appeal. The books of Daniel and Revelation are becoming the favorite scriptures of many and their visions are fantastically treated to fit our times. Premillennial and messianic voices multiply as the present social order seems settling into twilight. And while, as has been said, faith in specific social reforms is weakened among the thoughtful, all sorts of panaceas take quick though flimsy rootage in wayside minds. Many proposed remedies are more trivial than those suggested in the following conversation:

"Self-determination," one of them insisted.

"Arbitration," cried another.

"Cooperation," suggested the mildest of the party.

"Confiscation," answered an uncompromising female.

I, too, became intoxicated with the sound of these vocables, and were they not the cure for all our ills?

"Inoculation," I chimed in. "Transubstantiation," "alliteration," "inundation," "flagellation," and "afforestation." [5]

Verily the voices now crying in the wilderness constitute a "conversation at midnight."

If it be true, as Carl Sandburg has said, that "the earth is strewn with the exploded bladders of the puffed up," it

[5] Logan Pearsall Smith: *More Trivia*, Harcourt, Brace & Co., p. 41.

is also true that the earth has been strewn with skeletons of the despairing. Inflating pride is perilous, but so is paralyzing despair. Progress depends on man's power to dream and his faith that dreams will come true. When he comes to believe that progress is unreal, he ceases to pursue ideals. When he loses faith in man, democracy is done for. James Truslow Adams returned from Europe a few years ago, saying that America's greatest contribution to the world was the American dream, which he defined as the dream of a land where life shall be richer and better, with opportunity for every person according to his ability or achievement. We shall be caught by some dream again. The dilemma and despair of the people create the challenge of the prophet.

2. *Bewildered Youth*

When one has lost his way, it is the part of wisdom to recall if possible the point where he left the trail. Since group travel covers a wide terrain, there are several paths to be observed. Let us look first to our bewildered youth.

A young man in a New York parish recently put his predicament pretty vividly in words like these: "The earliest memories which I can recall are those of cutting out war pictures when I was a boy. Then I was sent to school and college in the hectic, booming 1920's, graduating from Harvard in 1929. That fall I was thrown into a depression. I have never yet lived in what you would call 'normal times.' What I need is something to believe in, something to hold to."

When we seek to get behind all the causes which produced that mental unsettlement, we are a bit like George Macdonald's pathetic little hero who tried to get back of the north wind. The fathers have sown the wind, and the youth are reaping the whirlwind. After the release from the war tension of twenty years ago, there was a moral relaxation, resulting in erotic fiction, extravagantly spiced pleasures, orgies of gambling in business, and the other ills that flesh was heir to in the 1920's. If it be true that children in the cradle are "tattooed with the beliefs of the tribe," it is also true that children in the jazz era caught the tunes of thought and feeling which jingled in their parents' minds. Furthermore, those parents had been so fed on propaganda that they suspected hidden motives behind everything and their resistance to the propagandists tended to make their children tonally deaf to the prophets.

If all youth could have the home discipline enjoyed by the late John Buchan and if all had his responsiveness, then the school would be as little needed in the clarification of faith as it was in his case. He tells us in *Pilgrim's Way* that his philosophy of life was shaped in his home. His school merely helped him to tidy up his tenets of belief and make them more orderly. But such adequate home influences are tragically rare. More and more responsibility is placed on the school for furnishing the framework of faith. With what result?

When the young leave their homes for the seats of higher learning, Mr. Adler of the University of Chicago charges that they come under the influence of a materialistic science, or "scientism," which turns morals and religion to dust, with the result that the campus resounds with ethically sterile words like "efficiency," "scientific," "objectivity" and "ideology," but is unresponsive to value terms like "right," "wrong," "justice," "brotherhood," "conscience" and "ideals."

Whatever the causes, it may be said that youth are characterized by ethical confusion, in that they are unsure

whether morals are more than *mores;* by aesthetic confusion, in that they have many tastes without much disciplined discrimination; by religious illiteracy, in that they
lack an understanding of the commonest Biblical refer-
ences, to say nothing of their rich religious heritage.

In their confusion, the young are listening for voices in
which they can believe. They are weary of mere waywardness. Faded is the Freudian emphasis on self-expression
which sent the young bloods roistering down the highways
heaving dead cats at all things sacred. Gone is the carefree
attitude of the jazz age, symbolized by the rollicking song:
"We don't know where we're going but we're on our way."
That spirit might be all right for a picnic, but life now is
no picnic. They are looking for the clues to life's larger
meanings.

Listen to these lines written by a young lad of sixteen,
my own son William:

"Our op'ning eyes have looked upon
    The fires that consumed the lost generation,
    And on each new horizon, we discern
    Old Chaos, wagging shaggy head,
    And hear his laugh amid a bloody dawn.
    We see, as you saw not, our fathers in your childhood,
    That by each man the ghost of failure walks,
    And that this ghost shall plead the better case
    Before life's arbiter.
    We have been born, our fathers, in a time
    When Progress means but wild experiment,
    The symptom of despair." [6]

In a day when it was less needed, the school and college
assumed the responsibility of providing a spiritual philoso-

[6] Quoted from Class Poem by William P. Sockman. The Hill School
Commencement, 1936.

phy of life. The first seal of Dartmouth College contained the motto: "*Vox clamantis in deserto*," with figures symbolic of Religion and Justice. Columbia University, through its first President, declared: "The chief thing that is aimed at in this college is to teach and engage the children to know God in Jesus Christ and to love and serve Him in all sobriety, godliness and righteousness of life." [7] How definite and determinative were those concepts in the early days of America's higher education. But with the increasing secularization of education, there has come a bewilderment in the minds of educators themselves. President Hutchins of Chicago confesses: "Our confusion is so great that we cannot make clear even to our own students what we are trying to do." University instruction has become so encyclopaedic in volume that annual catalogues of our large institutions rival in bulk the catalogues of a mail order house, such as Sears, Roebuck and Company. But the student, lost in the maze of courses, is in danger of learning "the price of everything and the value of nothing."

Modern secular education treats the transmission of religious tradition as either unnecessary or untouchable. Thus, it leaves an enormous vacuum where until a few decades ago our colleges placed the main emphasis of education. And with what is the vacuum filled? Walter Lippmann says: "It is filled with the elective, the eclectic, the specialized, the accidental and incidental improvisations and spontaneous curiosities of teachers and students. There is no common faith, no common body of principle, no com-

---

[7] Cf. "Christianity must be made the element and principle of all education. Where it has been laid as the first stone and acknowledged as the governing spirit, it will take up into itself, assimilate and give a character to literature and science. Where revealed truth has given the aim and direction to knowledge, knowledge of all kinds will minister to revealed truth." J. H. Newman: *Tamworth Reading Room*, Chap. 3.

mon body of knowledge, no common moral and intellectual discipline. . . . We have established a system of education in which we insist that while every one must be educated, yet there is nothing in particular that an educated man must know." [8]

Yet the graduates of these modern schools are expected to govern themselves, form civilized communities, clarify the social conscience and shape public policy. Where are they to find their directive purposes and steadying loyalties? As one graduate put it: "College gave us spokes but no hub. We came away with knowledge but no purpose, and therein is our dilemma."

In appraising the attitude of youth, we must beware lest we be led into easy generalizations. There is no average or typical student. The various youth groups whose pronouncements appear frequently in the press may be vocal minorities not at all representing the larger areas of thought, and perhaps only serving as sounding boards for adult leaders. Many spokesmen for youth fit Hosea's description of Ephraim, "Gray hairs are here and there upon him, but he knew it not." [9] While on every campus there are some serious students of world problems, others are concerned only with their security after commencement. While many are straining their eyes to scan the social horizon, probably more deserve the label bestowed by one college president, "blind followers of empty slogans." While some strive to break the vicious circles involving us in social evils such as war, others with craven conformity follow the customs of their clan. While some are on the spiritual alert hungrily feeling for the grounds of faith, others are undisturbed in

[8] Address before the American Association for the Advancement of Science, University of Pennsylvania, December 29, 1940.
[9] Hosea 7:9.

their traditional outlooks, or ignorant of changing view-points, or indifferent to the whole question of religion. While it is commonly said that the younger generation is impatient and even hostile toward organized religion, nevertheless the traditional young people's societies within the Church continue to grow.

Despite these diversities, there are certain general observations worth noting. Increased student attendance at campus religious services indicates a widening and deepening spirit of quest. The focus of interest in student discussion groups has shown a shift from social ethics to religious issues.

There are signs that the questing spirit of serious-minded students is being caught by college faculties. At present religious apathy seems to infect a larger proportion of professors than of students. But the seriousness of the situation is arousing university leaders. In his inaugural address, President Seymour of Yale declared: "We betray our trust if we fail to explore the various ways in which the youth who come to us may learn to appreciate spiritual values. . . . The simple and direct way is through the maintenance and upbuilding of the Christian religion as a vital part of university life." Significant of the same trend is the following sentence from the report of Princeton's president, accepted and approved by the university trustees June 10, 1940: "Princeton's historic position and present conviction and the acute needs of the time demand that we take vigorous steps to meet our responsibility of developing in our students a fuller understanding of religion and its significance."

And what is the significance of religion in the bewildering maze of secular studies? To develop disciplined free personalities equipped to function in our complex high-powered world; to inculcate not a skeptical temper of mind which believes nothing, nor a cynical temper which believes only the worst, but a critical temper which asks relevant questions and insists on pertinent answers; to deliver youth from soft-headedness by hard thinking and from coldness of heart by warmth of sympathies; to reveal the things that are worth living for and worth dying for; to impart dynamic motives which make fellow workers in creative social efforts and not sideline spectators of others' struggles; to organize in each life a hierarchy of values so that lesser loyalties are oriented and absorbed in one unifying goal of God's Kingdom—these are among the tasks which confront the spiritual guides of bewildered youth.

3. *The Wilderness of Work*

When the young go out from home and school "to make their living," the wilderness of moral and spiritual confusion thickens. They move into a world of work which in its frank appeal to the motive of individual advantage and in its basic principle of competition makes the pattern of life not a game but a battle. Every day the tension seems to tighten. The struggle for existence grows more exacting. Weaker men are pushed down and good men find it harder to rise. The centralization of power puts too great a strain on its possessors and leaves too much insecurity and uncertainty for the losers. The go-getter ideal of individualistic success creates an atomistic society as inadequate as a communistic order. Conscientious persons in church pews are baffled by the discrepancy between the beautiful ideals of the Master and the brute facts of the market place. And in a business order so engrossing that it is said "men go home to their offices in the morning," the goals toward which they drive six days in the week are likely to look more real than those set before them on the seventh.

If men would sit down and think it through, they would glimpse the trails to truth in this wilderness of work. They would look for the meanings of life beyond the means of living. "Religion is what the individual does with his own solitariness. If you are never solitary, you are never religious." [10] But in the modern tempo we take so little time to be alone with ourselves, to say nothing of being "alone with the Alone." The cultivation of individual solitude is a first step to the solution of our social problems. To some, such a statement will seem starting at the wrong end; but if we are to channel the rushing streams of industrial power, we must step from the turgid currents which turn the dynamos and look into the quiet waters where we catch the reflections of ourselves and of the heavens above. The guides in our world of work must be shepherds who can make us stop our devouring acquisitiveness and *lie down* in green pastures. They must lead us "beside the still waters." They must restore our souls.

Although we do not practice the solitude which makes for social understanding, nevertheless we live more and more in crowded loneliness. Oft repeated is the statement that the world in becoming a neighborhood has grown less neighborly. Races and nations are being brought closer together in space and time, but the increasing nearness sharpens the sense of difference. This principle applies within the local community as within the commonwealth of nations. The small town in which I grew up was divided by the railroad track into "the right people" and the others; the city where I now live is crisscrossed by countless lines

[10] A. N. Whitehead: *Religion in the Making*. The Macmillan Company, p. 15.

of demarcation. Here we live in larger numbers but relate ourselves to smaller groups. In addition to racial, economic and social distinctions is the segregation due to specialization. Even when we meet in the same church, we are an aggregation of doctors, lawyers, business executives, teachers, engineers. Narrowed by our specialties, we fall into the errors of experts. We lack the largeness of outlook and the breadth of sympathy which link us to the whole and thereby fulfill our own personalities. "For individuality signifies unique connections in the whole." [11] "Nobody is anything except as he joins himself to something. You cannot be a whole unless you join a whole. This, I believe, is religion." [12]

But how relate specialized and class-ridden individuals to a whole? To liberate their minds from petty provincialism through cultural understanding and widening world outlooks; to help men who are expert in their own lines to weave those lines into the patterns of a more symmetrical social fabric; to reveal the deeper experiences which underlie the departmentalization of work; to chart the areas of faith and hope and love wherein the specialties must meet; to convince competitive individualists that life consists not in the abundance of their belongings but in the greatness of what they belong to—such is the baffling but alluring challenge which confronts the modern spiritual guide.

The world of work is now so organized that the bare physical hungers of men can be satisfied with increasing ease. Before the dislocations of the present war pitched millions again into the shadows of starvation, western culture was achieving an economy of plenty. The cravings

[11] John Dewey: *Human Nature and Conduct*, Henry Holt & Co., p. 331.
[12] Bernard Bosanquet: *What Religion Is*, The Macmillan Company, p. 12.

for food and sex—commonly called our basic hungers—
have not in themselves caused the restlessness of the present
world disorder. It is not actual physical hunger that has
turned Europe into turmoil and set Japan and China at
each other's throats. No, it is a mixture of many motives—
desire for power, for a place in the sun, for imperial prestige,
for lucrative markets, for personal liberty, for the feeling
of social equality, for the right to happiness—these are
among the human hungers which have been capitalized to
arouse men to war. Here then is one of the tragedies of our
time. In a day of mechanical productivity when the physical necessities of men can be so easily supplied, the higher
hungers are asserting themselves, only to be perverted into
the lowest channels of misguided and brutal attempts at
satisfaction.

To interpret to the world's workers their own wistful-
ness; to take the higher hungers now hatching from the
chrysalis of drudgery and help them to wing their way to
the loftier satisfactions of the spirit—that is the glorious
function of those who would be guides to God. The lengthened leisure given by the machine and the sense of baffle-
ment produced by world chaos combine to create a matrix
from which a religious awakening might well be born.
Alas, at the moment, the warmakers are lessening the leisure
and increasing the chaos.

4. *The Encompassing World Chaos*

When we lift our gaze from the world of work, we see
ourselves surrounded by a world at war. And this seems to
add the last barrier of moral and spiritual bewilderment.
We must view personal and national duty in a more fluid

has been learned that Satan cannot cast out Satan, but the faith is not yet accepted that we can trust the Beatitudes to withstand a blitzkrieg. Gone is the old cocksure reliance on economic reform as the road to redemption, and the pulpit rings with the evangelical note, "Back to God"; but with many who utter it and hear it, that slogan is more an emotional release than a spiritual increase. Men are still moved by the fervent appeal, "Come to Jesus," for the figure of our Lord looks ever more alluring amid the fallen idols of our day, but thoughtful persons are asking where do we go with Christ after we come to Him? The popular evangelism of a few years past may still satisfy certain types of mind, but the more serious thinkers are not content merely "to brighten the corner where you are." They want to know what is around the corner.

The impression given to outsiders by a church leadership, confused and uncertain, may be gauged by the question posed in September, 1940, to a convention of social scientists: "Where are we to find a new religion that is as strong as the Protestant religion that was and the religion of nationalism that is? Such a new religion, with a new set of symbols, a new set of slogans, is needed to put across our education for the harmonious man." [15]

6. The Road Map

When the late Ramsay MacDonald was welcomed at the New York City Hall, he based his response on Michael Fairless's little book, *The Roadmender*. He stressed his desire to be a maker and mender of roads, opening out the way for human aspirations and human feet through the

[15] Professor Edward C. Tolman in a presidential address before the Society for Psychological Study of Social Issues reported in the *New York Times* Sept. 4, 1940.

coming generations. To be a roadmaker is not only the laudable desire of every leader; it is the rôle which makes him a leader. The explorer may pick his way through the wilderness bent only on discovery and unconcerned about any path for those who follow. The guide, seeking for himself and his immediate party a way out of the wilderness, may go around obstacles without removing them. But the genuine religious leader, true to the John the Baptist tradition, is more than an explorer searching for the mysteries of God, more than a guide helping lost and lonely pilgrims out of the City of Destruction across the Slough of Despond. He is the voice of one crying in the wilderness, "Prepare ye the way of the Lord, make his paths straight. Every valley shall be filled and every mountain and hill shall be brought low; and the crooked shall be made straight, and the rough ways shall be made smooth; and all flesh shall see the salvation of God." [16] The true minister of God, whether ordained or unordained, is called to be a roadmaker.

For this task in our time there is need first of all for a road map. Religious living is a quest as well as a conquest. If we are to overcome evil with good, we must get back to the fundamental question: What is good? Some of the socially accepted maps of life, like the map of Europe, have been ripped up into the fragments of a jigsaw puzzle. Life in a meaningless world is intolerable. A hand-to-mouth existence may satisfy the tramp who begs his morsels of satisfaction from the backdoors of life, but the sons of God want to know whither the road leads. Some years ago, Albert Schweitzer inveighed against the spirit of our age which drives us into action without allowing us to attain any clear view of the objective world and of life. It keeps

[16] Luke 3:4–6.

us in a sort of intoxication of activity without reflection on what this restless sacrifice of ourselves really has to do with the meaning of our lives. "And so we wander hither and thither in the gathering dusk formed by lack of any definite theory of the universe, like homeless, drunken mercenaries." [17]

A much-discussed weakness of contemporary democracies is that they have convinced their citizenry of no great objectives. This weakness of the "free peoples" has played into the hands of certain dictators who have galvanized their cohorts into action by creating a sense of destiny. A Nordic myth, however it may inspire Nazi marching youth, is not adequate to sustain morale for life's long pull. Nevertheless, for the time being, even such a flimsy artifice gives a sense of direction which democracies during the last decade or two have failed to impart.

Chesterton in his preface to *Heretics* says: "We think that for a landlady considering a lodger it is important to know his income, but still more important to know his philosophy. We think that for a general about to fight an enemy it is important to know the enemy's numbers, but still more important to know the enemy's philosophy. We think the question is not whether the theory of the cosmos affects matters, but whether in the long run anything else affects them." [18] These lines are being written in lovely Honolulu, the "Paradise of the Pacific," at whose portals stands a mighty concentration of ships and men, like the flaming sword at Eden's eastern gate "to keep the [American] way of the tree of life." But the surest defense of a nation is a sound philosophy of life, and the nations which

---

[17] Albert Schweitzer: *The Decay and Restoration of Civilization*, The Macmillan Company, p. 47.
[18] Gilbert K. Chesterton: *Heretics*, John Lane Co., pp. 15–16.

will ultimately win the present world revolution are those who have it.

For some years secular education has been hugging to its bosom the principle that its function is to teach youth how to think rather than what to think. While that emphasis has served as a wise corrective to sectarian, dogmatic and regimented thinking, must it not be supplemented by some guidance as to content? To teach a boy to think without giving him any guidance in what to think and then to turn him loose in the medley of modern voices is about as risky as to teach a lad to eat without giving him any guidance in what to eat and then to turn him loose in a well-stocked delicatessen. The boy is likely to die of indigestion before he learns a balanced diet. It is not restriction or regimentation to give road maps and guiding principles. These are the means of freedom. "Men, who are driven by their nature as living creatures to act, are also compelled by their nature as free spirits to relate their actions to, and bring them into conformity with, some total scheme of meaning, and are furthermore prompted by the dimension of their freedom to seek for an ultimate source of meaning." [19]

The free, full life comes only through living for large ends. Purposeless living is the worst of all imprisonments. Is this whirling planet a giant flywheel on which we are caught like sick flies taking a dizzy ride, or is it "a vale of soul-making" in which we, the sons of God, are working out an immortal destiny? What is history? "A tale told by an idiot full of sound and fury, signifying nothing"? Or, despite its vicious circles of recurring wars and its evident deterioration at many points, is history the travail of the whole creation bringing to birth a better order? What are

[19] Reinhold Niebuhr: *Religion and the Modern World*, University of Pennsylvania Press, p. 91.

the purposes worth working for? Why sacrifice for others? Why be good? Why live? Until such questions are faced, one has no working philosophy of life.

To be fellow seekers with men until they find a satisfying and saving philosophy of life is the rewarding function of God's guides. To show men that they exist in a frame of reference which is more than human, and are governed by a reality that transcends themselves, and are supported by an administration which guarantees the triumph of personal and spiritual values—that is the high privilege of God's roadmakers.

7. Lights for the Journey

Along with the road map a second equipment essential to God's roadmaker is adequate light. We are not only in a wilderness, but it is night.

Some years ago on a rainy Sunday night in Scotland a minister was leaving the home of his host for the railroad station. A lantern was given him and by it he was enabled to pick his way among the puddles along the slippery road. But when he rounded the corner and the station light came into view, it served as a great additional aid by giving him the direction. We need both lights to guide us in this night of the soul. And God's roadmaker is possessed of the Word which is both "a lamp unto our feet," enabling us to safely pick our steps, and "a light unto our path," giving us direction.

In our concern for world conditions we must not look slightingly on the small spheres of love and duty which immediately surround us. In *Cavalcade*, Noel Coward traces the fortunes of an English family through the first two decades of the twentieth century, from the time of the

Boer War when the young husband and father was sent
into the South African campaign, to the tragedy of the
Titanic wherein one son was lost, and on down to the
World War when another son was killed on the eve of
the Armistice. Then he pictures that household listening to
the triumphant London throngs as they celebrate the victory of England and her Empire. The grief-stricken mother
turns from the window to say, "My world isn't very big." [20]
At first sound that might seem a stultifying remark. No
Christian has a right to live encased in a small world, walled
against the heart throbs of humanity. But in another and
very real sense, our aliveness to our little personal world
prepares us for the exigencies of the world at large. The
immediate and intimate sphere is the vestibule through
which world issues come vitally home to us, and it is also
the verandah from which we look effectively out on the
world's problems.

It was the coördination of these two spheres that accounted in part at least for the genius of Lincoln. When
he was a young lawyer sitting behind the stove in Spring-
field, he visioned the impact of slavery on a whole nation.
Then when he sat in the White House as President, he saw
with intimate insight how the war affected the boys back
home. The long view gave him perspective; the short view
gave him sympathy. To keep the two in proper balance is
an imperative need of our time. In lengthening our world
outlooks, we often tend to dull our local sensitivities. The
modern Pharisee easily falls into the error of the proverbial
fool whose "eyes are in the ends of the earth." [21] The headlines stir our wrath against the dastardly deeds of distant
dictators, but such indignation, however righteous, does

[20] Noel Coward: *Cavalcade*, Part II, Scene 6.
[21] Proverbs 17:24.

not work for our redemption unless it drives home the questions: Does power ever go to our heads? Are we truly democratic in the circles of our authority? Can we use power without abusing it? The sins of certain labor leaders in our time of national emergency have recently aroused the public conscience to a point where preachers draw applause by denouncing them, but such preaching has little transforming power unless it presses home to the comfortable pew the question: Do we also take advantage when we have a chance to squeeze? Discussion of tragic foreign affairs frequently becomes only a mental cocktail giving a temporary fillip to jaded dinner guests. Denunciation of distant evils is one of our most devilish pulpit diversions, giving congregations the exhilaration of a false righteousness. Pious and frequent repetition of the prayer, "Forgive us our trespasses," may leave our hearts unharrowed by genuine repentance. Collective sinning is a dire reality, but collective repentance is usually too diluted to be curative. Our sinfulness does not really come home to us until it is translated into the first person singular.

Let us therefore keep alight the lanterns of faith, hope and love which illumine our immediate steps. Not only do they bring home to us the world's grave concerns but they serve to lead us toward the larger social solutions. When we cannot see the distant scene, we can still have the leading of a "kindly light amid the encircling gloom." A situation is seldom, if ever, so baffling that we cannot see at least one step ahead. To be sure, there may be a hundred confusing issues confronting us, but we are not centipedes, compelled to take a hundred steps at a time. We are bipeds and most of us are bright enough to know which is the better foot to put forward. And as Carlyle said, "Do the duty which lies nearest thee which thou knowest to be a duty. Thy second duty will already have become clearer." [22]

We might well recall a principle of progress which was revealed to me in my youth when I took up the study of geometry. I have a habit of opening a new book at the back and thumbing it through from the rear. Hence when I purchased a new text book in geometry, I opened it at the back, and my eye fell on a most forbidding looking object called a parallelepiped. It had so many diagrammatic lines and angles and letters that I said to myself, "If this is geometry, it just isn't for me." I would have given up in despair at that moment. But when my teacher took me in hand, he began at the first of the book, with the simple axioms, such as, "a straight line is the shortest distance between two points," and gradually we worked up from the simple problems to the parallelepiped. There is a homely philosophy back of that experience. One reason for our despair in so many situations and in the present world disorder is that we try to peep at the last page before we learn the simple axioms. We want to see how a situation is coming out before we learn the principles by which we should go in. We desire to see the big complex solution before we do the duty nearest at hand.

Dr. Washington Gladden, one of the authentic social prophets of the last generation, was a sturdy worker for world peace, racial brotherhood and industrial justice. There were times, however, when he was baffled by the complex problems. But although he could not read the last pages of those social solutions, he did say this:

> I know that right is right,
> That it is not good to lie,

[22] Thomas Carlyle: *Sartor Resartus*, Book II, Chap. IX.

> That love is better than spite
> And a neighbor than a spy.
>
> In the darkest night of the year,
> When the stars are all gone out,
> That courage is better than fear,
> And faith is truer than doubt.[23]

Those are axioms of moral conduct. Those are next steps which we can take when we cannot see the distant scene.

Yet with all our lanterns of faith, we come to those corners where we need to see the station lights which give the long directions. The religious leader must keep lifting the eyes of men from their preoccupation with the ways and mechanisms of living to see the meanings and ends of life. The ambassador of God has a duty to ask governments what they will do with victory when boys are asked to die for it. Do we seek to preserve the so-called inalienable rights to life, liberty and the pursuit of happiness? But what do we mean by life? Do we mean what Christ called the life that is life indeed? What is liberty? Is it freedom to do as we please, license for the irresponsible and the powerful, or is it the ability "to use and obey the laws of one's own nature," the liberty for which Christ set us free? What is the pursuit of happiness? Does it mean two cars in every garage or loving and livable lives in every home? Is it self-indulgence, a round of empty pleasures, or is it the blessings listed in the Beatitudes? Such are some of the leading questions which the prophetic voice in the wilderness has the right and the responsibility to ask. Even if we cannot give the complete answers, it is a real service to ask the right questions. And in the light of the Divine Questioner of Nazareth, we shall ultimately see light.

[23] Washington Gladden, *Ultima Veritas*.

CHAPTER II

A REED IN THE WIND

But what went ye out for to see, A man clothed in
soft raiment? Behold, they which are gorgeously ap-
pareled, and live delicately, are in kings' courts.
                                        LUKE 7:25

In eternity there is indeed something true and sublime. But all these times and places and occasions are
now and here. God himself culminates in the present
moment and will never be more divine in the lapse of
the ages. Time is but the stream I go afishing in. I
drink at it, but when I drink I see the sandy bottom
and detect how shallow it is. Its thin current slides
away but eternity remains.
        HENRY THOREAU, *Where I Lived and What
                                I Lived For.*

A REED IN THE WIND

John the Baptist was no sycophant, no private chaplain to the privileged. His sturdy independence stood four square to the passing winds. He was not a weathervane, but a guide-post.

The roadmaker who takes to himself the commission of Isaiah, "Prepare ye the way of the Lord, make his path straight," should have nothing in him of Ibsen's Peer Gynt, for the pulpit gives dangerous scope to any traits which point in that direction. Peer Gynt's falsification took subtle and polite forms such as begging the question, beclouding the issue, dodging the point, or calling hard facts by their softer synonyms. When scruples arose in his mind, he had a facility for evading the moral point and slurring it over with rhetoric. Whenever a situation became a bit too hot for him he would leave it. Rather than look into the face of stern realities, he would drug his spirit with restless activity. Peer Gynt refused to make the path of his own mind straight.

The pulpit, we repeat, offers all too many facilities for the Peer Gynt proclivities. The preacher may start out with the boasted integrity of Shakespeare's character who said, "I am a plain blunt man and speak straight on." He may speak on but not always straight; and his plain bluntness may take on a so-called tact and polish until it can be said of him what Bernardo del Nero said of Tito in *Romola*, that "he gets employed everywhere because he's a tool with a smooth handle."

The world pays tribute to the church by seeking the pulpit's support for almost every secular cause; but it takes a terrific toll from the church when it lures her preachers as spokesmen for so many secondary and even spurious causes. Felix Adler once thanked God for the truths which had used him. But it is one thing to be used of truth; it is another to have one's voice and office used to give temporary mental fads the semblance of divine truth. A minister may have the independence to resist a single royal patron, even as John the Baptist defied Herod, and yet barter away his soul piecemeal in the modern wilderness of popular patronage.

1. *Mortgaging the Minister's Soul*

While these chapters are designed for all who aspire to be God's guides, lay as well as clerical, the next few paragraphs are aimed very pointedly at the pulpit. We could wish that they might escape the laymen's gaze. And yet unless the pew is made alert and responsible, there is little hope of remedying the situation. When the woman of the street sells her soul, the law allows the purchaser to go scot free. Such perversion of justice should not have its parallel in the churches. When the man in the pulpit sells his soul, we should recognize that there is a responsibility in buying as well as in selling.

The pulpit is in more danger of selling its freedom through catering to the public than of losing its liberty through governmental pressure, real as this latter peril is. The selling of the soul is such a subtle process in any sphere, and especially so in the realm of spiritual leadership. A man may spurn the idea of selling his soul outright and yet suc-

cumb to the temptation of mortgaging it. The minister is
ordained to preach the word of God as sincerely as he can
know it. But what good is it to proclaim God's word without those willing to listen? Is not a half-truth given to a
full church of more value than "the whole truth and nothing but the truth" given to the faithful dozen who have
sworn themselves to sit like a jury on Sunday nights before
the minister, no matter who he is? And since people prefer
a religion which makes them feel safe and good rather than
right and real, why not make one's sermons palatable to
the public? And do not those who come get so much more
out of a sermon when the crowd is large? Thus we can go
on rationalizing. In trying to put our message across to the
people, it is so easy to allow our concern for its reception
to dull the edge of its thrust. Forty years ago Ian Maclaren
declared that in former times the indispensable quality of
a sermon was its soundness of doctrine but in his day the
essential test was that it should be interesting. How much
harder does the pulpit now strain to heighten the interest
of its sermons in order to catch the ear of our hurrying
generation amid all the siren voices competing for attention. And how often the contents of doctrine, aye even of
truth itself, are submerged in the efforts at popular appeal.

On every side we hear it said: "If the church would give
us what we want, we would attend its services." In a religious journal,[1] a specialist in business salesmanship essayed
recently to advise the pulpit how it could reach a larger
public by appealing to the twelve basic emotional hungers
which the business world capitalizes. He listed these hungers as follows: security, progress, health and beauty, su-
periority, companionship, acquisition, activity, competition, group urge as in family and race, curiosity, sex, and

[1] *Zion's Herald*, March 13 and 27, 1940.

religion. That people will go where they think these hungers can be satisfied, is not to be denied. That cults outside the church frequently capitalize these desires on a frankly egocentric basis will also be admitted. That certain preachers within the church are successful salesmen to self-seeking patrons is also well-known. But let us remember that it is one thing to cater to popular hungers, it is another thing to feed the soul through them. In making a numerical success of their Sunday night services, some ministers boast that they lure the people through the motive of curiosity, desire for entertainment and other more or less selfish appeals. Then having corralled the crowd on the lower level, they lead their hearers up to the plane of high religion. No doubt this can be done. But such services do not always have a lifting or lasting value.

People think they know what they want; they do not always know what they need. And the minister's task is to lead men from what they want to what they need. Our very terminology today reveals a certain betrayal of this trust. We speak of a minister being called to "serve a congregation." We seldom, if ever, speak of a minister being called to "save a congregation"; or if we do, we mean that he is called to save the church property. When the congregation becomes the norm by which sermons are measured, a minister has put a mortgage on his soul.

The process of losing control of one's soul is still more subtle. We can sell our free souls by merely keeping silent. Thomas Wolfe has a sarcastic line, "As it was said of a certain famous Bishop, 'he had a large and easy swallow.' " [2] In swallowing we use some of the same organs as in speaking, but the direction is different! To swallow and be silent

[2] *The Web and the Rock*, Harper & Bros., p. 234.

saves many a situation. But our Lord was more interested in saving souls than situations.

Silence has its merits. In the ministry there is the silence of gentlemanly reserve, like that of our Lord before the woman brought to be stoned. There is the silence of modesty, when we refuse to speak on subjects beyond our knowledge. There is the silence of integrity, when we decline to mouth affirmations of which we are not convinced. There is the silence of reverence which is owed to persons as well as to divinity. The good minister of Jesus Christ does not rush noisily into the privacy of other personalities nor should he take upon himself the divine function of shouting from the housetops what has been told him in secret, even when he omits names and uses it only for homiletical purposes. The homiletic urge may be a divine endowment but it can sometimes do devilish tricks. It has to be watched lest it lead to the use of things sacred to others. We should remember what the little boy wrote in his essay on Socrates: "Socrates was the wisest of the ancient Greeks. He knew everything about everybody, and he told everything he knew, and they poisoned him!" The minister cannot long remain the trusted confidant of the people if he becomes the publicizer of their sanctities, even under the smoke screen of preaching. Yes, silence is golden when prompted by modesty, or reserve, or kindness. But too often men discover that silence is golden because it pays professionally.

A man may have too much self-respect to run away from a moral fight after it has begun; and yet he may be so discreet as to stay away from the fighting zone. A minister may preach a searching sermon against the inhumanity of the priest who passed by the wounded victim of the robbers, and yet he himself may have become accustomed to taking the safer roads to Jericho. Clarence Darrow at a convention of newspaper editors once made the charge that every editorial office had some "sacred cows" which were kept immune from criticism. Every preacher should search his mind to see if there be any subjects which he has been avoiding through fear. It was said of a certain diplomat that he knew how to be silent in six languages. Cowardly silence can be so easily rationalized as diplomacy or discretion; yet as Robert Louis Stevenson said, "The cruelest lies are often told in silence." [3]

To make up for such timid silence, a minister may shout loudly on safe subjects. When certain social issues, like war, are found to be too sensitive for pulpit handling, the preacher can always fall back on vehement denunciations of vicious plays or salacious books, since there are usually not many playwrights or authors in his pews. Organized vice and organized crime are also pretty useful targets. And even organized labor is a convenient target for preachers who wish to curry favor with comfortable congregations. Long-range shooting at absentee sinners is a temptation of those too timid for straight-from-the-shoulder combat. And some ministers with a dogmatic manner and a clever discrimination get a reputation for courage by attacking safe subjects. They merit Thackeray's biting description of Dean Swift: [4] "His servility was so boisterous that it looked like independence." It is amazing how slow the pew is in detecting false courage!

The preacher must beware lest even his pastoral consciousness dull the edge of his prophetic conscience. A good

---

[3] *Virginibus Puerisque*, Chap. IV.
[4] *Great Short Biographies of Modern Times*, Alfred and Charles Boni, p. 1016.

pastor writes his sermons with his parishioners in mind. But he should make sure that it is their needs rather than their desires which he is watching. There is ever the danger of tempering the wind to the shorn lambs—in fur coats! And to change the figure, he should learn from the aviator the value of the headwind. A tailwind speeds the plane along when it is up in the air, but for landing and rising the pilot heads into the opposing wind. And unless the preacher wishes to stay up in the air he too must head into the opposing currents of interest. No sermon lands effectively on the field of a sinful heart unless at some point it opposes the trend of that heart's earthly desire. And no sermon rises to saving height unless it sails against the current of the world's low-born wishes. When Nicodemus on a Palestinian house-top listened to our Lord liken the Spirit of God to the sighing of the wind, he no doubt saw the point; but the trouble with the timid scholar was that he was looking for the tailwind rather than the headwind. Hence Nicodemus never took off nor made a landing with the Galilean. The true preacher of Christ is not "a reed shaken with the wind" of the world, but a pilot rising with the wind of the Spirit.

Francis Bacon's "*idola* of the marketplace" still bewitch and bedevil the presentation of the Gospel. By this term Lord Bacon meant the errors due to the intercourse of man with man. Supposedly we clarify our views by speech and conversation. The exchange of ideas should serve to correct false impressions and break down barriers of misunderstanding. But how often human intercourse only adds to the confusion. We echo the catch-phrases of the crowd. We repeat rumors. We capitulate to names and badges. We are led astray by clever slogans. Recall how Caiaphas, the hostile high priest, argued for the crucifixion of Jesus.

"Know ye not that one shall die for the many in order that all perish not?" [5] Those words constitute the very formula of the Christian theory of atonement, and yet they were used by an arch enemy of the Christ. Thus language can be twisted to distort truth.

The preacher must ever strive to preserve his medium of speech from profanation by the *idola* of the marketplace. The profanity which Jesus denounced was more than the mere vulgar vice of swearing, as we know it. It was the deeper profaning of speech by insincerities. He said, "Let your communication be, 'yea, yea'; and 'nay, nay.' " [6] The Master would have his followers mean what they say and say what they mean in the simplest and most straightforward way. And the pulpit has a special responsibility to set the style in sincerity of speech. As the colonial pulpit was the chief school in which Patrick Henry and others learned the language that shaped the American Revolution, so the contemporary pulpit should generate an atmosphere of honesty whose contagion would help to remove the insincere and unreal elements which pollute our polite social intercourse, poison our diplomacy and often corrupt our business dealings.

One of the most damning descriptions of a preacher is sometimes wrapped in what superficial persons regard as a compliment. How often it is said of a popular pulpiteer, "He is a good actor." Dramatic ability is an asset to any speaker, and the minister's message, dealing as it does with the issues of life and death, of hope and love and destiny, has in it the deepest elements of drama. But the preacher is a messenger not an actor. The actor is applauded for his art: the herald is remembered for his message. The only

[5] John 11:50.
[6] Matthew 5:37.

dramatic art appropriate to the pulpit is artlessness. And this is attained and preserved by keeping in the company of the simple, the genuine, the elemental. Supreme among these sincerity-restoring factors is the Christ himself. Jesus does for the minister somewhat as Uncle Pio did for the singer in Thornton Wilder's *The Bridge of San Luis Rey*. Uncle Pio had discovered the singer in a cheap music hall. He trained her until she became an opera singer of merit. But her shallow nature continued to be too easily content with the crowd's applause. If the public approved, she was satisfied with even a mediocre performance. But when she turned from the cheering crowd, there was Uncle Pio waiting for her in the wings of the stage. She could not fool him. She could not win his approval with anything cheap. He saw her for what she was—but still believed in her. So Christ stands in the wings of the pulpit.

A physical aid, which one minister has found helpful, may be worth passing on. In the room from which he enters the pulpit he has hung his favorite portrait of the Christ. Before going forth to face his congregation he stands gazing into the eyes of his Lord; and then again before leaving the church after the service he stands in front of his Master. It is one thing to pronounce a benediction in the name of the Lord Jesus Christ: it is another to receive a benediction from the One in whose name we have spoken. And only as the preacher feels that presence and faces that stern yet loving appraisal is he preserved from being "a reed shaken with the wind."

2. *Caught in the System*

The modern guide to God is not a lone voice in an untrammeled wilderness but a leader amid a meshwork of precedents. Forerunners have followed lines of least resistance until the codes of conventional conduct resemble the streets of downtown Boston. The compass of conscience seems an inadequate guide in threading the paths of Christian duty through the complex situations of our day.

The Christian movement in becoming an institution became involved in the financial and political systems of the social order. The minister as representative of the church must operate within these social structures. Sometimes a situation is so bad that the only way to save one's soul is to pick up and leave it. Old Trader Horn, whose salty philosophy and independent spirit made him a refreshing literary figure a few years ago, said, "The first thing education teaches you is to walk alone. Aye, you can sure stand on your own spear when you have learned the word 'good-by' and can say it clear." And our Lord on more than one occasion made his protest felt by walking out. The world needs for its progress those pilgrims who, like John Bunyan, pick up and leave the City of Destruction.

But while we can sometimes save a situation by saying "good-by" to it, we cannot leave a system so easily. We can quit a certain line of work, but it is hard to quit the whole business system. We can leave a particular church in protest against its program and policy, but can we effectively abandon the church which is the body of Christ, the world's hope of redemption? Bunyan's *Pilgrim's Progress* is not a complete program for those who seek a better world. We need a Citizen's Progress. Christ's counsel is, "Ye shall be in the world but not of the world." How to live in the world without losing hope in its redemption, how to stay in the systems without surrendering to their compromises, how to get along with one's crowd and yet to get the crowd along—those are among the challenges involved in guiding men to God.

The Christian gospel is now faced with the challenge of controlling the social currents which it helped to start. Christianity began among the lowly. The manger is a true symbol of its social origin. But when the spirit of Christ lodges within a life, he sets forces at work which tend to make the person socially potent. The spirit of Christ enters a man who is shiftless and makes him industrious. He comes to a person who is enslaved by his appetites and makes him master of his passions. He transforms the fellow who is dishonest into the reliable, trustworthy employee. The Christ stirs a mind which is asleep and awakens it into alertness.

Therefore these traits of industry, sobriety, honesty, alertness and their like begin to change their possessor's place in society. That is what happened to the early Christians in the Roman Empire. They became such good artisans and craftsmen that they attracted the attention of Emperor Constantine who legalized their religion, and in two or three centuries the despised Christian sect became the social and civic leaders of the waning empire. Similar was the case of the English Puritans. The sober industriousness inculcated by piety made the followers of Cromwell the founders of England's financial structure. The same results are to be seen among the Quakers around Philadelphia. Their honesty and fidelity to principle proved a business asset and established the foundations of large fortunes. Something of the same thing has happened wherever the teachings of Christ have been planted. With all its emphasis on charity and "treasures in heaven" it has set in motion a law of accumulation which makes for treasures upon earth.

It is no accident that the western culture which developed in the wake of the Bible's spread is more dynamic than the oriental civilizations. The scriptural teaching that man is a worker together with God for the Kingdom, that man has a fighting chance and is not chained in fatalism, that man is to seek the truth which shall make him free— these are among the roots which gave rise to the spirit of science, inventiveness and adventure, characterizing the countries of the Hebrew-Christian religious tradition. And in view of this, it is not surprising that the modern cult of success has identified godliness with prosperity, and has sought to find in Christ's teachings a pious basis for current business methods, interpreting our Lord as the long-neglected super-salesman whose principles would vitalize the sluggish markets of Wall Street.

The Christ, whose earthly career began at the bottom and whose teachings men have used to raise themselves to the top, now finds little room for himself at the top or the bottom of the social scale. The treatment accorded to Christ in the formative circles of business, society and politics is somewhat similar to the status of a grandfather who has transferred the management of his property to his children. The grandparent is given a place at the table. He is shown a certain deference due to his age. But he is outside the main currents of the family's activities. The real business goes on without him. The modern contrast with the medieval dominance of religion is apparent when one recalls that until the sixteenth century, economics was only a branch of ethics, and ethics of theology. Dean Gauss of Princeton may be judging the current too much by straws on the surface, but nevertheless his observation is pertinent when he argues the waning prestige of religion from the fact that the clergy are practically never considered for federal political office. This fact, he maintains, suggests more than the separation of church and state. A religion, he holds, which has been excluded from politics, business, science and public education—from all those fields which mean most to a modern man—has lost influence and power.

Such a charge may be countered by the assertion that in a democracy religion exerts an increasingly potent influence through public opinion; that while we do not elect clergymen to office, officials are very alert to seek the opinions and the support of church bodies. We may say too, that the American conception of the church differs from that of Europe. In a European town the parish church or cathedral dominates the landscape, standing amid the surrounding buildings like a mother hen among her brood. In our American towns and cities the church edifices are dwarfed by the business structures alongside. But our churches, be it remembered, cultivated the soil which nourished the luxuriant crop of secular developments. Like the Son of Man, his church in America came "not to be ministered unto, but to minister." Like the salt of the earth, it hides itself in the substance which it savors.

Nevertheless, the church is now being tested as to its power to control the political, economic and social forces which it helped to generate. It confronts the expanding regulations, even the totalitarian tendencies, of nationalistic government, the demands of economic pressure groups, the aloofness of organized labor, the suspicion and censorship of capitalistic interests which support it. The Christianization of these group attitudes is far more difficult than the conversion of individuals. But the church cannot be reconciled to leaving moral man in an immoral society. The church will lose even its power of personal evangelism if, having once caught the social vision, it should go back to an individualistic gospel of merely saving men out of the world. The shepherd who shows himself too weak and timid to tackle the wolves of this world will hardly be trusted as a guide to the realities of the next world. Deserted and despised will be the church which seeks only to save boys in Sunday School without essaying to keep them from being brutalized. "The problem of Christian politics is one of life and death for our times. The evils overwhelming the world today are exactly the final result of the idea current in the classic age according to which politics cannot and must not be Christian because it is a pure technique, an art intrinsically independent of ethics and religion, and whose only law is the quickest material success by any means at all, provided only they are efficacious." [7] "The moving finger writes, and having writ moves on." The church has written a chapter of the Kingdom program in the days of Maurice, Kingsley and Rauschenbusch. It may now correct that chapter. But it cannot tear it out. The church of Christ must work for the salvation of group life or lose its power to save individual souls.

3. *Some Guiding Principles*

If we are to prepare a highway for our God, we must project the old personal virtues up to the new social frontiers. The subtlety of our temptations has outrun the sensitivity of our consciences. The Ten Commandments have not been repealed, but like old traffic laws they do not restrain modern speeders. As in the days of James Russell Lowell:

> In vain we call old notions fudge;
> And bend our conscience to our dealing;

[7] Jacques Maritain: *Religion and the Modern World*, University of Pennsylvania Press, 1941, p. 16.

The Ten Commandments will not budge,
And stealing will continue stealing.[8]

But we must lengthen the range of imagination and interpretation if we are to make the regulations of Sinai reach "the ramparts we watch." A man might have honesty enough to keep straight in the simple man-to-man dealings of a village bank or a country store and yet not have integrity sufficient to resist the subtler temptations in the ramified dealings of long-range corporate business. A gentleman might abhor the thought of participating in a holdup and feel no twinge of conscience in taking dividends from a throttling monopoly. If we are to teach honesty adequate for our time, we must gear it to Wall Street as well as to Main Street. One high-placed powerful, unsocial executive may do more damage than a dozen drunken derelicts. A person may be too puritanical even to mention the seventh commandment and yet pay wages which encourage his salesgirls to break it. "Thou shalt not bear false witness" may restrain a man from violating his oath or lying about an acquaintance, yet he may join in vicious propaganda against a whole people. And the old commandment, "Thou shalt not kill," must now be discussed in terms of nations, not merely of neighbors.

Along all these lines culture has begotten a social consciousness: but that is something far less than a Christian conscience. The poignancy of personal sin has not yet penetrated our participation in social evils. And until it does, social redemption will lag. When we as individuals feel as John Donne felt: "Any man's death diminishes me, because I am involved in Mankinde; and therefore never send to know for whom the bell tolls; It tolls for thee." [9]

[8] Motto of American Copyright League. Written November 20, 1885.
[9] *Devotions*, No. XVII.

When the Christian so identifies himself with the sins of his group that, like his sinless Lord, he is willing to be baptized for their redemption—then, and then only, shall we make real headway in extending the highway of God into our corporate life.

This sensitizing of the social conscience comes not through the shocks of war or other calamity, but by cultivation. Awareness of the world's brutalities may merely bruise our feelings. Or the radio, the press and the motion picture may remind us so repeatedly of the world's sufferings that we grow callous to them. Or the badness of men may beget a mood of condemnation which prevents the spirit of repentance. The rapid means of communication make a daily impact which tends to change the thought habits of church folk. Our godly forefathers were accustomed to open and close the day with periods of private devotion in which the gaze of God came home to them as directly as the path of light comes across a lake from the setting sun to the feet of the watcher. Such moments left them mellowed and repentant.

But we in contrast quite usually begin the day with the morning paper and end it with the last news broadcast, both of which turn our minds toward not our own sins but the crimes and misdeeds of others. The result is that the hours which to our grandparents were times of repentance become to us periods of condemnation. We are in the mood of shooting at the villains on the screen; but if we would destroy the evils which produce the dictators and the other sinister figures which shadow our world, we should strike at the evils in the heart. Our tendency is to kill the sinner and keep the sin; Jesus, on the other hand, fought the sin and loved the sinner. Twenty-five years ago we killed the Huns and then helped rebuild their war spirit. "We may fight against what is wrong, but if we allow ourselves to hate, that is to insure our spiritual defeat and our likeness to what we hate." [10]

Anger eases the conscience but does not eradicate the evil. And it is easier to inflame men with destructive emotions than with constructive ones. It would seem that emotions like fear and anger and hatred lie near the surface of our natures and are very inflammable. And it is always a temptation for the minister to follow the line of quickest response. Mass meetings can be multiplied if they are of an "anti" nature—against some nationality, some race, some "ism." But meetings to sponsor Chinese relief or milk for English children meet less popular response. More than ever in my memory, men are now in the mood where they can be rallied around their hates so much more easily than around their loves. It is the same psychology which brings thousands to see a man knocked out in a prize fight while only a few medical students go around to the hospital the next day to see him put together again. If we make our pulpits prize-fight arenas, we can be sure of a crowd for a time at least. But "fighting parsons" must beware lest they too become reeds shaken with the wind of popular passion. The gospel of redemptive love is betrayed by militant and popular preachers who court King Demos as well as by the comfortable sycophants whom the Master condemned as "living delicately in kings' courts." In a democracy Demos is quite as dangerous as Midas in corrupting the pulpit. Compassion is harder to arouse than passion, but much more necessary, at least now.

We must release the spirit of grace to match the spirit of wrath. We cannot quite define how we create an atmosphere, yet we know its reality. We know that a home,

[10] AE, *The Living Torch,* Macmillan & Co., p. 351.

a school, a church, and at times a nation, is imbued with a spirit, which may be subtly but potently effective. And we know, too, that one person can sometimes determine the spirit of a home, and a consecrated Lord's dozen can create an atmosphere for a large church. Written large on the wall of a certain railway station are these words: "Strength is not in the majority but in the sincerity of the will to sacrifice." What should be remembered is that living cells have a power of infecting the body politic with love as well as with hate. And while anger and hatred and fear are quickly inflammable, love and courage have the longer glow. Love "beareth all things, believeth all things, hopeth all things, endureth all things. Love never faileth." [11] Love is the Christian's *absolute*.

4. *Love Amid the Relativities*

"Love alone can transform itself according to the concrete demands of every individual and social situation without losing its eternity and dignity and unconditioned validity." [12] Accepting the absoluteness of love, the Lord's roadbuilder is faced with the problem of projecting its implications amid concrete situations and conflicting loyalties. How far the motive of love falls short of reducing moral conduct to a multiplication table of abstract exactitudes is seen in the pronouncement of the Oxford Conference: "It is our absolute duty to do what is relatively best."

In charting what is "relatively best," we have two foci of vision: the sovereignty of God and the sanctity of individual man. When we fix our eye on the former we rele-

[11] I Corinthians 13:7.
[12] Paul Tillich: *Religion and the Modern World*, University of Pennsylvania Press, p. 56.

gate rival deities to a subordinate position, freeing ourselves
from their claim to be final arbiters of the conscience. When
we keep our eye on the sacredness of personality, we treat
men as ends in themselves and not as eggs for Napoleonic
omelets or as pawns for social programs; we cry out whenever and wherever we see human beings hurt, whether
or not we have a cure to offer.

But the "sovereignty of God" may be stressed into a
Calvinistic predestinarianism or a Barthian social paralysis,
and the "sanctity of personality" may lead to a coddling
and sentimental individualism. If they are to be vital and
wholesome, these terms must be translated into reverence.
"Reverence for the eternal is the first thing in knowledge."
And reverence for personality is the last word of love.

When we try to define reverence, we catch only the
echoes of reality. It is too deep for words. Therein lies its
gripping power. A traveler, let us say, enters Westminster
Abbey. As he walks down the dim aisles, he finds himself
in the company of historic names. The greatness and dignity of the human spirit begin to lay hold on his imagination. From the shadowy vaults and arches, a sense of the
centuries descends upon him. Things invisible and eternal
engulf the things that are seen and temporal. The dead
seem close to the living. The divine seems near to the human. The visitor's voice sinks to a whisper. The little noisi-
ness of his thought is hushed with awe. That is an experience of reverence.

Reverence is higher than fear. It is fear lifted above
self-interest. It is love enriched with awe. It keeps the fear
of God from becoming paralyzing and the love of man
from becoming stultifying. It restrains the ego but ex-
pands the spirit. It is rooted in the shadowy numinous but

it grows with enlarging knowledge. "Reverence," as Carlyle said, "is the divinest thing in man." [13]

The inculcation of reverence is basic to all our programs of social improvement. The secularization of life has stripped the soil of society as the greed of man ploughed the grassy western plains and transformed them into a dust bowl. We have been suffering the moral dust storms resulting from destroyed sanctities. Dr. C. J. Hambro, Norwegian delegate to the League of Nations in 1935, wrote, "Here in Geneva we have every fear but the fear of God." [14] The roots of reverence must be sunk again. The primary injunction of all social action, "Thou shalt love thy neighbor as thyself," has no measuring value or impelling force to one who has lost reverent regard for his own personality. Statute laws may be turned out by the tome but they will not insure a law-abiding society unless men are held by inner sanctions which underlie legal restrictions. "Character," said a wise counsellor, "is what a man is in the dark." Our complex and corporate society has developed a new darkness—that of the crowd. As the group grows, the individual responsibility and moral initiative tend to shrink unless sustained by sanctities which keep a man straight when no one is looking. The practice of requiring oaths may be extended, as it now is, to insure loyalty to the American way of life, but oaths have no binding power on persons devoid of reverence for honor and truth. Without a deepened reverence for man, multitudes will go on singing "God bless America" with sentimental fervor, and then turn to denouncing their fellow Americans as immigrant ingrates, impossible Jews and hopeless morons.

[13] *Sartor Resartus*, Book II, Chap. 2.
[14] Quoted in *The Christian Century Pulpit*, March, 1941, p. 50.

One dilemma of democracy is that so many who shout for it deny the human dignity on which it rests.

Thus reverence for God and man is the soil on which Christian democracy and kindred social programs grow. To cultivate this reverence is not a simple or sudden process. As the secularized and sordid Jacob heard the divine injunction, "Arise, go up to Bethel and dwell there," [15] so our generation must get back to its Bethels and dwell there —back to the spots where, as to Jacob, God seemed very real and heaven came close to earth. To frequent the shrines of worship where symbol and sacrament help God to break through the clouds of our unknowing; to relive in memory the luminous moments of our own youth when the insights of innocence and purity flashed upon us; to listen with veneration to the wisdom of life's veterans who have lived long and well; to cultivate the mental comradeship of the noble dead; to lift our eyes from the social chaos to the fidelities of nature until we feel a "Presence that disturbs (us) with the joy of elevated thoughts; a sense sublime of something far more deeply interfused"; [16] to look at our fellow men until we see beneath their foibles, their futile strivings, their cruel contortions and feel

> there is something here
> Unfathomed by the cynic's sneer,
> Something that gives our feeble light
> A high immunity from night;
> Something that leaps life's narrow bars
> To claim its birthright with the hosts of heaven.[17]

[15] Genesis 35:1.
[16] William Wordsworth: "Lines Composed a Few Miles Above Tintern Abbey," lines 94–96.
[17] James Russell Lowell: "Ode Recited at the Harvard Commemoration, July 21, 1865," lines 91–96.

—these are some of the paths by which we can return to our Bethels and revive our reverence for the sovereign God and the sacred personalities of his sons.

The sincere seeker after the path of love amid the relativities is not left without historic help. One there was who held the course of absolute love for God and man through the conflicting loyalties of life. While the program of Jesus for our complex contemporary situations cannot be dogmatically defined, the directions of his motives are clearly discernible. Definitions change, but directions are eternal.

There is a *Jesus way of life* which is independent of the conditions under which it is lived. It is a way which can be followed by the humblest peasant as well as by the most profound scholar. It is a way of reacting to one's environment whatever the environment is. Jesus dealt primarily with the way a person looks at things and not with what he looks at. When he said, "Be not anxious for the morrow," "Give to everyone that asketh thee," "Whosoever shall smite thee on thy right cheek, turn to him the other also," he was telling men what should be their sound spontaneous reactions to the world. The validity of these commands is not vitiated by the apocalyptic emphasis which holds that Jesus shared the current expectation of the world's approaching cataclysmic end. Nor is the authority of Jesus' ethics undermined by the eschatologists with their emphasis that our Lord did not intend the Beatitudes as a working order for this world but rather as the blue prints of a superhistorical society. Jesus was laying down the basic motives and spontaneous reactions of life, whether the time be long or short, whether the realm be here or there.

Working from within out, Jesus' first interest was with man as subject, with man as doer of good, rather than as receiver. Henry Cadbury deserves a hearing when he says

Jesus' concern is not so much the saving of society as a society of saviors.[18] Having this emphasis, Jesus did not give specific legislation for social institutions, such as government, taxation, the war system, inheritance, and the like. But he did deposit a leavening motive which inevitably lifted the crust of restricting institutions. The Sabbath is made for man and not man for the Sabbath. The State is made for man and not man for the State. The world is made for man and not man for the world. Yes, even death is made for man and not man for death. And yet in all this he thought of man as the doer of duties rather than as the recipient of rights. The preservation of personality requires an outgoing emphasis rather than an ingrowing one because the paradox of life is that the individual gets what belongs to him only by giving himself to what he belongs to. Jesus imparted a spirit which soon runs counter to current conventions and suffers repeated crucifixions, but is resurrected repeatedly into something greater. Thus the Jesus way of life remains the same yesterday, today and forever. Being the incarnation of love, it is as absolute as love itself.

The Jesus way of life, thus conceived as a set of spontaneous reactions, becomes the norm by which the Christian tests his motives amid the relativities of a contemporary situation, however complex it may be. Take, for instance, the most tense issue of our time, that of the Christian's relation to war. No horror of war, no outrages on the part of hostile peoples, can repeal Christ's law of love. If the individual feels that his motive of love can be most effectively expressed by helping to kill some that more may be saved; if he can conscientiously participate in the killing process without hating the persons slain; if he is convinced that love has no alternative means of working its will; then—

18 Henry Cadbury: *The Peril of Modernizing Jesus*, Macmillan, p. 116.

and then only—for him it is his "Christian duty" to fight. We must make allowance for the limitations of our own judgment, for even the best of us, like Paul, see "through a glass darkly." We know the absolute God and the absolute duty of holy love, but our knowledge of God and love is not absolute.

When we strain too hard to foresee consequences of our adherence to a Christ-like motive, we lessen the force of the drive; we are so likely to lower the direction into mere expediency. The Christian takes his stand in scorn of consequences to himself; sometimes he must take his stand in scorn of consequences to others, trusting that when he fixes his position in line with the Light of the World, his shadow of influence will fall in the right place. If we go around always looking for the consequences of our conduct, we become afraid of our shadows. Furthermore, our finite wisdom cannot foresee nor follow the full results of our deeds for we work with a God who "hath chosen the foolish things of this world to confound the wise," a God who "hath chosen the weak things of the world to confound the mighty," a God who "hath chosen the things which are not to bring to nought the things that are." [19]

In the hands of a God who outdistances our wisdom and in the face of problems which outrun our wits the Christian must get his ethical bearings more and more from looking at his Lord and less and less from looking at the presumable social consequences of his course. In doing so he may for a time be denounced as a poor parent or as a disloyal citizen. But the testimony of experience is that the person who with his best intelligence and sincerest conscience takes his stand in loyalty to Christ's absolute of love has never proved

[19] I Corinthians, 3:27, 28.

thereby an unworthy parent or a poor patriot. Loyalty to Christ safeguards the lesser loyalties.

During the World War the Ninety-first Psalm was called the aviator's psalm because it begins by stressing the advantage of altitude: "He that dwelleth in the secret place of the most High shall abide under the shadow of the Almighty." The highest position is the place of the most power. That is quite as true in the realm of the spirit as in the realm of aviation. He who takes the highest moral position in his attitude toward war or any other social issue, he who heroically holds his lofty level of principle in scorn of immediate appraisals and inviting expediencies—he will be in the place of the most spiritual power tomorrow, if not today. This principle of moral altitude explains the almost universal respect accorded the Quakers.

The ethical absolute is a "real" in morals somewhat as infinity is a "real" in mathematics. Perfection cannot be attained existentially. But it is an "impossible possible"; aye rather, it is an *impossible necessary*. It is a paradoxical truism that when we strive expectantly for the things we cannot do, we are enabled to do better the things we can do. "A man's reach should exceed his grasp, or what's a heaven for?" [20] Heaven gives the glory of going on toward the goals unattained here. But is the Kingdom of Heaven, which Christ bade us seek, only the superhistorical aftermath of attainment? It makes a vital difference whether we view the Jesus way of life as an earthly goal lying beyond our day's march or whether we regard it as a heavenly mirage designed merely to lure travelers across the desert of this world. Personally I cannot view Christ's promise of the Kingdom as a mirage in the sky. I believe we belong to

[20] Robert Browning: "Andrea del Sarto," lines 97–98.

the succession of those who "having obtained a good report through faith, received not the promise; God having provided some better thing for us, that they without us should not be made perfect." [21] We are in the relay race of the aspiring but imperfect. "Wherefore let us lay aside every weight and the sin which doth so easily beset us, and let us run with patience the race that is set before us looking unto Jesus, the author and finisher of our faith." [22]

5. *The Timely and the Eternal*

How far are ethical absolutes affected by the times in which they are proclaimed and applied? "Ye have heard it said by them of old times . . . but I say unto you . . ." is a formula which recognizes that "Time makes ancient good uncouth." There is a fullness of time when ideas come to ripeness and fruition. There is a timeliness essential to effective effort in any realm. The timing of shots is as important in the pulpit as in presidential fireside chats. The guide to God must steer through current issues and his message must take cognizance of them. As Mrs. Henry Hitt Crane said recently in introducing a speaker: "He is steadfastly old-fashioned in his convictions, superbly modern in his ideas and startlingly ahead of his times in his ideals."

There is a tendency, however, to exaggerate the uniqueness of current situations. Times are less variable for preaching purposes than we commonly assume. The carnal mind is still at enmity against God; man is still so ignorant that he needs prophecy; he is still so rebellious that he needs a master; he is still so guilty that he needs atonement; he is

[21] Hebrews 11:39, 40.
[22] *Ibid.*, 12:1, 2.

still so helpless that he needs a Savior. The basic heart hungers call for the same bread of life. Preachers may take the phrasing of their subjects from journals of the day, but the substance of their message should be based on the timeless rather than the timely. In the words of "AE" we must turn from the "politics of time" to the "politics of eternity."

The task of the preacher is to lift men above the low views of their times, to give them the elevation and outlook which enable them to distinguish currents from eddies. A sound historical sense is one of our most needed stabilizing forces. Men need to be reminded that "in an important sense, nothing has been changed, though everything has been interrupted. One would not go on listening to Beethoven if one's house were afire, but the beauty of music remains no less beautiful because our listening to it must be postponed." [23]

A young student was recently discussing her college major. She was considering art, but she remarked that to specialize in art at a time of such world turmoil seemed a case of fiddling while Rome was burning; perhaps she had better focus on social science. Whereupon her mother reminded her that the social science which she had studied in college a generation ago is now outmoded, while the forms of art criticism are as true as ever. Art values remain although museums may be bombed and the ownership of paintings may be changed by conquest or revolution.

Yes, and the basic elements of Christian social science remain despite wars and revolutions. No amount of regimentation erases the fact that ultimately public welfare becomes actual in the private joys of single individuals. The common welfare is the well-being of individual men. Reverence for personality and the redemptive power of love

[23] Irwin Edman: *Candle in the Dark*, Viking Press, p. 16.

remain central to Christian democracy. Governments may grow frightened, as they now are, and say that force is the final arbiter. Religious leaders may join with the state and resort to the sword as the temporary tool of the spirit. But whatever nations do in emergencies, force is not the final arbiter. Love is the last word in the vocabulary of redemption. And when the guns have been fired and the boys have been killed, the issue, as Lincoln said, will not be settled until it is settled right. We can see the force of Edman's remark that "nothing has changed but everything has a new and desolating context." [24]

The emphasis of the religious guide should be on the abiding content rather than on the changing and desolating context. There are plenty of press columnists and other secular interpreters to survey the current scene. But there are too few who help men to lift their eyes unto the eternal hills, whence cometh our strength, our direction and our deliverance. On the September Sunday of 1939 when the current war broke on Europe, a minister was preaching at a summer hotel in upstate New York. To the stunned congregation he felt called to speak on "The Hills of God." He let his mind sweep the Biblical horizon, beginning with the Mount of Sinai where the ethical bases still show their enduring strata as on the Palisades of the nearby Hudson. He went on to the Mount of the Beatitudes where the grace of God clothes with verdure the stern outlines of law and justice; then on to the Mount of Transfiguration where the select disciples beheld, as it appeared to them, Moses and Elijah in communion with Christ, thus glimpsing the connection between the law, the prophets and the gospel; and on to the Hill of Calvary where love spoke its last word and vicarious suffering won its supreme victory. The lift

[24] *Op. cit.*, p. 17.

of that large outlook and the sequence of the long vista made the minister, at least, feel with Madariaga that "Nations are formal, men and mankind are essential." [25]

To reveal the vistas of eternal values to men bogged in the Slough of Despond requires more than individual insight and prophetic inspiration. The institutional and sacramental aspects of the church serve as an even wider channel through which eternity breaks into time. Men turn to the church when life is most real to them, as in the times of marriage, parenthood, calamity or separation by death—and remember, this personal searching goes on regardless of wars and world revolutions. At such times the minister must be the spiritual telegrapher who can translate the flashes of the interrupted current into messages which comfort with the conviction of life's continuity. Franz Werfel, in *Embezzled Heaven*, contrasts the helplessness of the intellectuals with the assured poise of the poor serving woman when death invaded the little group. The former were adjusted to the smooth currents of superficial living, even to the eventualities of social change; but only the servant had a faith equal to the emergency of death.

The effort to adjust the eternal to the timely is fraught with certain perils. In reconstructing Christianity to fit current patterns of thought there is danger of devitalizing the eternal values. The Gnostics in the second century, the Deists in the eighteenth, Strauss and Feuerbach in the nineteenth all tried to acclimate Christianity in the intellectual atmosphere of their times. But "when we review the history of these efforts to adapt Christianity to current world-views and prevalent moods, we realize that they were more dangerous to Christianity itself than were the open attacks

[25] Don Salvador de Madariaga: *The Price of Peace*, Richard Cobden Lecture, May 8, 1935.

upon it which the times produced. Just because they were congenial to the spirit of their own age, they were attractive to the men who lived in that age and thought and felt with it. But though ways change as times go by, to the cool reflection of the modern man Gnosticism, with its hierarchies of coupled aeons leading up toward a lovely and knowable God, is as unreal as a nightmare. If any of these attempts at reconstruction had succeeded in winning the acceptance of all Christians, or of most of them, Christianity would have long since passed into forgetfulness." [26]

Persistent in every generation is the peril of trimming the eternal down to fit the timely. God's program and schedule of redemption cannot be reduced to the scale of Russian five-year plans or Nazi four-year plans or American New Deal plans. Specific reforms may be compressed and speeded by time schedules. And let us not deny their value. But let us not mistake specific social reforms for the Kingdom of God. The religious leader should give his aid to these but he should not give his gospel away to them. All our timely social programs are to be appraised and applied in the light of a divine plan: *the plan of the eternal God pursuing a redemptive purpose with an everlasting love working through the life and cross of an undying Personality.*

To keep paramount this eternal plan does not mean evading the emergencies of the timely. Rather it means filling the present with eternal value. One strategy of successful living is to live each moment to the full, not lessening its energy and enjoyment by regret for the past or anxiety for the future. Such was Jesus' way of living. Such is the mood often to be observed in unspoiled youth. To the boy

[26] C. M. Jacobs, *What Is Christianity?* The United Lutheran Publication House, p. 19.

immersed in a baseball game, that diamond is a little bit of heaven and those nine innings are a little block of eternity. This ability to crowd eternity into time is to be seen in the creative moments of artists and poets and scientists. In fact we all have some fleeting glimpses of eternal living, when time is forgotten. But how tragically we shut ourselves off from these windowsills of heaven by our imprisoning sense of time. We earthbound mortals in our anxious effort to have a "good time" have almost lost our capacity for living in the present. To vitalize the present and not to evade it is our reason for bringing eternity into time. In proclaiming the everlasting gospel, we seek to help men live an eternal present. "This is life eternal that they might know thee the only true God, and Jesus Christ, whom thou hast sent." [27]

[27] John 17:3.

Chapter III

A PROPHET

What went ye out for to see? A prophet?
LUKE 7:26.

> At your voice
> Panic, despair, flee away.
> Ye move through the ranks, recall
> The stragglers, refresh the outworn,
> Praise, re-inspire the brave!
> Order, courage return.
> Eyes rekindling, and prayers,
> Follow your steps as ye go.
> Ye fill up the gaps in our files,
> Strengthen the wavering line,
> Stablish, continue our march,
> On, to the bound of the waste
> On, to the City of God!
> MATTHEW ARNOLD, *Rugby Chapel*.

Chapter III

A PROPHET

1. *A Voice Not Our Own*

A Filipino delegate to the Madras Conference in 1938 reminded his hearers that in India the common way of testing the value of coins is to throw them on the floor or some hard surface to see if they ring true. "Christians," he said, "are being tested by similar treatment today. The world is throwing them down hard to see how much of good there is in them." And the ring of truth for which the world is listening must carry the note of divine revelation. Is the Christian message from God or only from men? That is the question.

The Filipino's test is echoed in the familiar *Fortune* editorial of January, 1940. The writer admitted that America owes its ideals to the church, but asserted that the church is not now leading in the mastery of our new material conditions. He chided the church shepherds with following rather than leading the flock, citing how the pulpits bent their messages to the will of the majority in the case of slavery a hundred years ago. The church, he said, is not inspired and the result is a vicious spiral of spiritual disillusionment. And this was his conclusion: "There is only one way out of the spiral. The way out is the sound of a voice, not our voice, but a voice coming from something not ourselves, in the existence of which we cannot disbelieve. It is the earthly task of the pastors to hear this voice, to cause us to hear it, and to tell us what it says."

Such a statement might be met by the quick retort that the preachers who resisted the voice of the crowd in the last war and clung to the voice of God, as they interpreted it, were relieved of their pulpits by the business-minded laymen who support such magazines as *Fortune*. But let us not allow the inconsistency of the pulpit's critics to blind us to the cogency of their appeal. The world is weary of guesses and speculations. It is tired of uncharted freedom and disillusioned about man's cleverness. Men want to hear about God. With some it is the cry of desperation, like that of the soldier in the trenches who said to Bishop McDowell before being ordered over the top: "What do you know about God—quick?" Or the hunger may be revealed in the haunts of the intellectuals. The very critical and rather worldly wife of a college president, describing the campus preachers of a certain past season, singled out one to whom she referred with relish: "He talked about God as if he knew Him."

The shift from preoccupation with social ethics to the age-old quest of our relation to God is apparent in the theological seminaries which I have observed. Whereas a decade ago the most popular courses were in the field of social problems, now they are in the department of theology. In Roman Catholicism the Neo-Thomist movement, in Eastern Orthodoxy the influence of Berdyaev, in Protestantism the significance of Barth and Brunner—all attest to the hunger for divine authority. We crave a faith which can speak in the indicative mood and not merely in the imperative or subjunctive. During the recent decades the approaches to the Bible have put the emphasis on man's activity and pushed into the background the idea of divine revelation. The Bible was regarded as the record of man's progressive religious experience; God was a sort of un-

discovered continent waiting for man's advancing explora-
tion. But the tide of interpretation has turned. Men sought
a good to love and now think of themselves as being found
by a good that loves them. From the seeking man to the
searching God is the shift of focus. Christianity stands ultimately by its claim to be the bearer of a divine revelation.

A distinguished Roman Catholic spokesman charges that
Protestants have squandered their spiritual patrimony in
prodigal fashion. In the sixteenth century, he says, they
gave up belief in the authority of the church; in the seven-
teenth century they ceased to believe in the authority of
Scripture; in the eighteenth they gave up faith in the divinity of Christ; in the nineteenth they relinquished the
belief in God as Judge; and in the twentieth they surrendered belief in the necessity of religion and obligation to
God. Again, let us not allow the irritating inaccuracy of
such a charge to lessen our determination to recover whatever valid bases of authority may have been lost. But the
point to be kept in mind is that these bases must be relevant
to all rational living. The only valid religious authority for
us is one that is acceptable to free and enlightened minds.
Dogmatic assertions may arrest attention by their air of
authority; they may look strong in contrast to the tentative
utterances of the uncertain; they win the following of those
who fear to question; but can they convince and convict
the minds that will make tomorrow? The presentation of
an inscrutable revelation which men are not competent to
criticise is dangerously parallel to the methods of political
dictators. And while the world in its weariness with uncharted liberty, is temporarily subject to the dictator complex, the roots of free thought have not been eradicated
and the future lies with the true liberals.

Some years ago the New York *World* ceased publication. It was credited at the time with having probably the best staff of editors in the metropolis. One explanation of its financial failure is worth pondering. The critic said that the *World* failed to hold its readers because it emphasized its editorial page to the neglect of its news columns; and the public, he went on to say, wants to know what is going on in the world but it does not wish to be told what it should think about it. The current vogue of the press columnists and radio news interpreters may seem to belie the statement that the public does not wish to be told what it should think. While we are so bewildered by contemporary chaotic events that we crave guidance, nevertheless we soon weary of those who are too pontifical or dogmatic in their interpretations. Reverence for personality includes respect for mental freedom. Such is the attitude of God in his gift of self-revelation; such must be the spirit of the prophets who interpret that revelation.

"Revelation is such knowledge of the divine will as cannot be found through submersion in myself or in the secret of the world, but comes through an act of communication, an act of personal self-impartation from outside our own range, in which God gives us himself." [1] Yet, gift of God though it is, revelation does not relieve the receiving heart from toil. Rather, it quickens and vitalizes the responding powers. It equips the receiving mind to understand what it remembers and to remember what it has forgotten. It is supernatural and yet it uses man's natural faculties. The divine nature within awakes to the knowledge of God and the knowledge of God awakes the divine nature within. It is beyond reason, yet it is relevant to the rational bases of authority. The prophet is the hearer of a voice not his

[1] Emil Brunner: *The Word and the World*, Scribner's, p. 21.

own, but he must bring his revelation to listeners who have the right and the responsibility to sift illusion from reality.

2. *How God Speaks*

The revived interest in revelation has led to several significant recent explorations of the field.[2] In studying the nature of revealed knowledge, we need not magnify the mystery of it. The surrendered heart does not mean the supine mind. "The wind bloweth where it listeth, and thou hearest the sound thereof, but canst not tell whence it cometh and whither it goeth: so is every one that is born of the Spirit." [3] Yet the mysteries of the wind served only to spur men to seek its secrets. So the call of the Spirit summons us to explore the channels by which it comes.

Consider the act of knowing. Begin with sense experience. I see an apartment house across the street. How do I know it is a house? I can see at most only two sides of the building at any one time from my stand on the ground. But a house with only two sides would not be a house at all. Hence when I say that I know it is an apartment house I must supplement what I can see through my eyes with what I can remember from having seen the other side, or with what I infer about its other sides, or with what I imagine. Thus knowledge by sense perception obviously depends upon a process of rational activity including memory, inference, imagination, synthesis and the like. And this rational activity is greater or less according as interpretation is needed to supplement sense-data and to complete their significance.

[2] Cf. Edwin Lewis: *A Philosophy of the Christian Revelation*, Harper & Bros.; H. Richard Niebuhr: *The Meaning of Revelation*, Macmillan.
[3] John 3:8.

How meager would be our knowledge if it were limited strictly to immediate sense experience and not enlarged by memory and belief and inference and interpretation. And these capacities of memory, belief, interpretation and their like are so integral to personality that we have a right to regard them as necessary factors in relating us to reality.

Man is a meaning-bearer. He looks at a thing and he says, "This means that," and the meaning becomes a reality to him. Man is also a time-binder. He remembers, and the memory is a reality to him. Man is also an experience-mediator. He may say of the house which he sees that he is certain it was honestly acquired. He did not actually see the transfer of property, but he has had evidence to convince him of the owner's general integrity. He therefore asserts that he has "reason to believe" that the building was honestly bought. This may be called mediate certainty in contrast to the immediate certainty of actual sense-experience. Religious certainty rests on both—on what one actually sees and also on what one has "reason to believe." Thus when Paul says, "I know whom I have believed," his certainty is based on what he had seen plus what he had interpreted plus what he had reason to believe—all of which were derived from capacities that are integral to personality.

In this act of knowing, the faculty of imagination plays a rôle which deserves more intellectual respect than is commonly accorded it. In our knowledge of nature we find it necessary to use imagination constantly in order that we may interpret the bits of sensation which come to us. The jostling mob of confused, unintelligible, meaningless visual and auditory sensations is made to march in order by a mind which approaches and apprehends them with some total image. We hasten to meet the sensations that come to us with anticipations of our own. We do not hear isolated ejaculations, separate and therefore meaningless words, but apprehend each sound in a context that we in part supply. By means of imagination we interpret as we sense, and sense as we interpret.

Furthermore the imagination at times becomes creative and with a leap of intuition outruns the leaden feet of logic. The poet's insight and the artist's vision are roads to reality even though they cannot be surveyed with the measuring rods of science. "Poetry," said Shelley, "redeems from decay the visitations of divinity in man." [4] Moreover, there is much resemblance between the scientist's flash of discovery and the intuitive insight of the artist, the poet, or the religious seer. The advance of science requires more than accurate observation and acute analysis. Up from the armies of laboratory testers rise from time to time those men with sufficient insight and imagination to transform data into discoveries. They are the seers of science. Others verify their theories with elaborate demonstration, but it is creative vision which projects the theories. When asked how he had discovered the law of gravity, Sir Isaac Newton replied: "By thinking about it continuously. I keep the object of my research constantly before me, waiting until the first light begins to dawn, little by little; finally this changes and at last the light is complete." [5] In our respect for science let us not overlook its debt to imagination and intuition. Let us not prostrate our supra-rational faculties at the shrine of cold reason. Observation, as well as synthesis, is sharpened by the subjective element. "It is not

[4] Percy B. Shelley: "A Defence of Poetry" in *Essays of British Essayists*, Colonial Press, 1900, p. 165.

[5] Louis Figuier: *Vie des Savants illustres*, Paris, 1870, translated by Barrett H. Clark in *Great Short Biographies of Modern Times*, Albert & Charles Boni, p. 713.

true that we observe best when we are entirely devoid of emotion." [6]

The subjective element in observation is apparent in the simplest situations. When two cars collide on the highway there are certain to be at least two different versions of the affair, and both usually very vocal. And when the traffic officer tries to settle the dispute by calling bystanders to witness, the confusion is often worse confounded. This subjective factor is enhanced the more the elements of value enter the situation. Take a conspicuous example. When certain Greeks came asking to see Jesus, as the event is recorded in the Fourth Gospel, the Master exclaimed: "The hour is come, that the Son of Man should be glorified. Verily, verily, I say unto you, except a corn of wheat fall into the ground and die it abideth alone: but if it die, it bringeth forth much fruit." [7] Then, according to the record, the realization of his impending sacrifice seemed to lift Jesus into an exalted mystical mood of prayer, saying, "Father, save me from this hour—Father, glorify Thy name." The report goes on, "Then came there a voice from heaven saying: 'I have both glorified it and will glorify it again.'" Here was indeed a revelatory moment. Something was happening in the soul of Jesus. But how did the bystanders understand it? This is the record, "The people, therefore, that stood by and heard it said that it thundered, others said 'An angel spake to him.'"

How is such divergence to be explained? Is one view objective reality, and the other subjective fancy? Is not the clue to be found rather in Richard Niebuhr's distinction between "external history" and "inner history"? [8] The

[6] A. N. Whitehead: *Religion in the Making*, Macmillan, p. 124.
[7] John 12:23, 24.
[8] Cf. H. Richard Niebuhr: *The Meaning of Revelation*, Macmillan, Chap. II.

case history of a hospital patient as kept by the doctors is very different from the autobiographical experience of the sick man as he climbs back up the road to health. Yet both are real and both are history.

When revelatory events occur, their recognition as divine revelation is always inner history. Case histories cannot be written of those experiences wherein prophets exclaim, "The Word of the Lord came to me." That exaltation in which Isaiah "saw the Lord sitting upon a throne, high and lifted up," was an experience which no reporter could photograph and no anatomist could dissect. So is it with our own experiences. One worshiper in the pew may hear the word of the Lord, while the man beside him will go out saying, "What was the preacher thundering about this morning?"

The approach to revelation therefore is by way of preparing the mood which can receive it. The mission of the prophet is to bear a revelation and also "to make ready a people prepared for the Lord." [9] It is the pure in heart who see God. But the purifying of the heart is as personal as the functioning of the eyelid in cleansing the eye. Purity of heart is singleness of vision and only the seeing self can make the eye single. Purity of heart means freedom from compromising and selfish motives, and only the inner self can control motivation. When the editor of *Fortune* summons the preachers "to hear a voice not our voice," he is challenging them to necessary spiritual attunement; but when he summons them, as he says, to "cause us to hear it," he must recognize that no one can open the door of another's heart to the divine voice. Tradition has it that Holman Hunt called in some friends for a preview of his painting of Christ at the door. After looking at the canvas,

[9] Luke 1:17.

one of his friends pulled the artist aside and called his attention to what seemed an oversight—there was no latch on the door. Whereupon Hunt reminded his guest that there can be no latch on the outside of personality's door. That door must be opened from within. The preacher, like his Lord, may bear witness unto the truth but only those who are of the truth hear the voice of revelation. "For this cause came I into the world, that I should bear witness unto the truth. Every one that is of the truth heareth my voice." [10]

In addition to observation, imagination, and intuition, there is a moral set of the soul prerequisite to capturing the revelatory experience. The condition is well expressed by Dr. John Mackay: "There can be no true knowledge of ultimate things, that is to say, of God and man, of duty and destiny, that is not born in a concern and perfected in a commitment." [11] There must be a concern for righteousness and a commitment to righteousness. The seeker must be looking *with* the seers and not *at* them. He must be craving to *be* something and not merely to *know* something. The will of God must have his vote before he can get its vision.

And that vote must be cast in the precinct of duty nearest to us at the moment. We all know of some one thing not right in our lives. We can begin by removing that. Thus we start to "walk in the light as he is in the light." When the light of understanding is too dim for faith *in* God, we can keep faith *with* God. Readers of A. J. Cronin's *The Keys of the Kingdom* will remember the touching scene where the priest is bidding farewell to the dying young doctor, who has given his life heroically in the Chinese

[10] John 18:37.
[11] John Mackay: *A Preface to Christian Theology*, Macmillan, p. 45.

epidemic. The doctor gasps, "I still can't believe in God." The priest in his effort to comfort replies, "Does that matter now? He believes in you." Later when the Mother Superior and the priest's own conscience chide him with the query whether he had said the right thing, he reasons thus: "There is one thing we most of us forget. Christ taught it. The Church teaches it . . . though you wouldn't think so to hear a great many of us today. No one in good faith can ever be lost." [12] Without endorsing all of Cronin's implications, we can say that keeping faith *with* God is prerequisite to a vital faith *in* God. Fidelity is the finest form of faith. And the testimony of experience is that we rise from certitudes of duty to certitudes of faith.

3. *Where God Speaks*

(a) *Through the Seekers*

After this preview of the approach to revelation, we look now at the places of revealing experience. Since moments of revelation belong to "inner history" and not to "external history," it is appropriate to speak confessionally in the first person. Familiar is the report that Henry Ward Beecher found many of his sermon inspirations while walking the city streets. Personally I cannot say that the sidewalks of New York have been especially fertile soil for sermonic seeds, but I must confess that one of the first places in which I find God revealed is in my fellow human beings. In my search for God's presence, I am helped by looking at the lookers. What started men on the trail of God and what keeps them on it? We can hardly explain the persistent longing on the ground of primitive fear. When we try to sum up the motives which send men in

[12] A. J. Cronin: *The Keys of the Kingdom,* Little, Brown & Co., p. 211 ff.

search of God, about the best we can do is to say that it
is their sense of inadequacy. Man does not feel himself
adequate to confront this world without higher help, and
moreover, he does not feel that this world in itself is adequate for his own highest development. In one sense the
world is too big for him; in another, it is too small. That
double sense of insufficiency persists in the thoughtful
modern as in the inarticulate savage. In fact, it grows upon
us with the progress of civilization. One of the paradoxes
of our time is that we have more power at our disposal
than ever before, and yet we seem more helpless than ever.

In the physical order we explain the instincts and apti-
tudes of creatures by saying that they are in response to
environment. The skin of the animal grows fur in conformity to the climate wherein it dwells. The sensitivity of
the eye develops in response to the light surrounding it. If
it is correct to assume that our physical appetites and ap-
titudes are called forth in response to environment, is it not
logical to say that the persistent universal search for God is
man's response to His presence? As Pascal put it, "Thou
wouldst not seek me hadst thou not already found me."
Our aspirations and ideals are not man's inventions but
God's revelations. The very despairs of mankind are eloquent evidence of His presence. We seek Him because He
first sought us. "He inwardly incites what he outwardly
crowns." God is in the hunger that sets men searching for
Him.

(b) *Through the Finders*

Furthermore I get evidences of divine revelation not
only in those who seek for God but also in those who find
Him. The fact that so much of this finding is inarticulate
enhances rather than lessens its evidence. The silent dignity
of mourners in the presence of death does much to redeem

funeral services from the paganism of those professional practices which still cling to such occasions, and also reveals to me that ingrained godliness which shows man more than mortal. The devoted scientists who would dismiss any least suggestion of saintliness but who keep sane while the world goes mad with hate and hysteria, who not only pursue the ideal of truth undeflected by dictators or utilitarian pressures but also are sustained by that ideal—these reinforce my hold on the promise: "When he, the Spirit of truth, is come he will guide you into all truth." [13] The uncomplaining bearers of physical pain who seem to possess the "peace of God which passeth all understanding"; the poets and artists who keep beauty alive in a dark and ugly world, singing gaily in the face of the gathering storm; the taxi-drivers and their like who under hard exteriors reveal so unexpectedly the milk of human kindness and show that the human spirit spreads despite the organized cruelty of governments—these are among the revealers of God. Since God is love, every act of loving is God in us. Since God is truth, every sincere search for truth is cooperation with God. The mystery of iniquity keeps me from any vague pantheism or Pollyanna liberalism. And the mystery of godliness is to me an abiding matrix of revelation.

For I can explain godliness in men only as the revelation of God. For me it is easier to account for evil in God's world than to account for goodness in a godless world. I can explain a bad man as a good one gone wrong, but a good man is somewhat more than an evil one in reverse. Hate may be explained as love turned sour, but love is more than sweetened bitterness. I can understand how God has to give His children freedom of choice and how some can

[13] John 16:13.

misuse their liberty into the excesses of a Hitler or a Napoleon; but if there be no God, I cannot understand why a man should lay down his life for his friends or why Christ should pray for His crucifiers. I can explain a hurricane as the orderly winds gone awry but I cannot account for the rainbow without the sun. The godliness which I see in men strikes me as the reflection and revelation of God.[13a]

(c) *Through Nature's Voice*

And what shall we say about nature as a source of divine revelation? Here honesty compels me to be modest, for my adult life, hemmed in by the cañons of New York, has lacked those wider horizons and lovely vistas with which nature has enriched the minds of those who keep her company. But when the mystery of iniquity threatens to overshadow the mystery of godliness, then nature serves to restore my vision. When the disorders of man's world dim the consciousness of divine control, the marvels of nature's orderliness correct the perspective. A bird's-eye view of human society reveals men and nations going around in the vicious circles of recurring iniquities and ruinous wars; but the birds who view such human chaos are themselves guided through the trackless air on their unerring migrations. The radio may shake our faith with the tragic news of accumulating disasters, but the radio itself is a revelation of "something far more deeply interfused whose dwelling is the light of setting suns, and the round ocean, and the living air." And when we are prone to doubt the goodness of a Divine Administration which allows the uncalled-for wrecking of homes, bombing of cities and breaking of bodies, we do well to remember that nature lavishes upon us adornments quite as uncalled-for as these disfigurements. The Creator who deprives men of what they seem to de-

[13a] Cf. Author's *Live for Tomorrow*, Macmillan, p. 61.

serve also gives so much more than men deserve. By what
right can man claim the magic splendor of an autumnal
forest or the purple grandeur of a sunset or the blanket of
wild flowers which spring lays over the grave of winter?
These are all God's extras, evidences of His abounding
grace. Yes, when society seems so senseless in its sinfulness,
we can look at the fidelities of nature and feel with Einstein
a "profound reverence for the rationality made manifest in
existence." [14]

Yet while nature yields these restoring visions of orderliness and bounteous grace, it does not give me the God
who speaks. It renews my faith in the fact of God; it does
not reveal the face of the God in whom it leads me to believe. Nature often guides me to God; but it does not give
me the guidance of God. For that I have to look further.

(d) *Through Mystical Insights*

There are times when earth-bound mortals get what
they call an inspiration. The narrow matter-of-fact work-
aday experience is suddenly flooded and transformed by
the inrush of a vast experience as from another world.
Something seems to break in upon the familiar tenor of our
thoughts. There seems to be an unexpected appearance in
the mind of something strikingly different from its habit-
ual course and general contents.

Nothing is more certain than that some persons at some
moments are carried beyond the usual range of their
thought and arrive at insights which seem to be given them
from a higher wisdom. Sometimes these flashes and insights come like sudden meteors which leave only a brief
train of fading light behind; and sometimes they come to

[14] Albert Einstein: *Science and Religion*, Address at Conference held
at Columbia University on Science, Philosophy and Religion, September 9, 10, 11, 1940.

persons able by their literary power to preserve them. "Those who have become the true children of God and are reborn of the Spirit . . . these receive from the Spirit of God many and various favors and activities. Sometimes, like guests at a royal feast, they are satiated with indescribable enjoyments; sometimes they are filled with a divine and intimate delight, like that of the bride when she rejoices in the presence of the bridegroom. . . . Sometimes they are seized by a lively compassion at the sight of human misery, and, in the ardor of their charity, they give themselves wholly to prayer and tears, begging the Divine Mercy for the whole human race. . . . At other times, he immerses himself in a profound silence; and then his soul enjoys great peace, and tastes in its quietude of ineffable delights. Or else the Holy Spirit illuminates his intelligence and communicates to him a supernal wisdom, and high knowledge which human speech cannot express. Thus does divine grace cause the incessant alternations of peace and of activity." [15]

When, however, we look a little more deeply into these flashes of inspiration, we find that they are not wholly intrusions from without; they seem to be a spark igniting something within the person. Daniel Webster, trying to tell later to a friend how he was able to speak for four hours on the meaning of the Constitution of the United States in his famous reply to Senator Hayne, for which he apparently had had no time for specific preparation, said: "It was perfectly easy: I stood up, when all of a sudden a smoking thunderbolt came by and I seized it and hurled it at Hayne." [16]

[15] Macarius, *Homily XVIII*, 7–9.
[16] Quoted in Rufus M. Jones: *Pathways to the Reality of God*, Macmillan, p. 158.

Of course that was a figurative and by no means a full explanation of what Webster did. No one else in the Senate that day saw "a smoking thunderbolt." (It might be well if sometimes our Senators did!) What happened was that the occasion released something which had been storing up in Webster's mind through long years of study. Through reading and thought, Webster's passion for the Constitution had been charging his mind, and the speech of Hayne was the occasion which caused the flash of the thunderbolt. The spur of the moment released the study of the years.

Thus flashes of inspiration come partly because of something electric or transcendent in the atmosphere and partly because of something immanent or charged up within us. Man's rational mind becomes a sort of conductor between the Oversoul and the Unconscious. He is carried away in the spirit. He is in the hands of One "able to do exceeding abundantly above all that we ask or think according to the power that worketh in us." [17] "It shall be given you in that same hour what ye shall speak. For it is not ye that speak but the Spirit of your Father which speaketh in you." [18]

In such moments a man is looking *with* the seers, not *at* them. In those luminous moods preaching rises to the heights of prophetic utterance. Yet one cannot preach about them, nor can he make clear to others the steps by which he reached his assurance. Intuition leaves no footsteps whereby others can follow. Sermons on the Holy Spirit usually go over the heads of congregations, and even sermons about prayer often fail of practical value. We can no more describe the *how* of mystical insight to others than Jesus could explain to Nicodemus the evidence that he was

[17] Ephesians 3:20.
[18] Matthew 10:19, 20.

"a teacher come from God." All he could say was, "The wind bloweth where it listeth, and thou hearest the sound thereof, but canst not tell whence it cometh and whither it goeth: so is every one that is born of the Spirit." [19] When the lad asked the old sailor "What is the wind?", the old salt replied, "I can't tell you, but I know how to hoist a sail." A congregation does discover when a minister knows how to hoist the sail to catch the winds of the Spirit, and they do feel "the power from on high" when he preaches with it rather than about it.

This mystical communion is the greatest single need of the contemporary pulpit. It can be cultivated, even though it cannot be analyzed. A woman of my acquaintance who has been going through deep personal sorrow, has immersed herself in the writings of Evelyn Underhill, Baron von Hügel, and mystics of earlier date. She has learned the secret of entering into the stillness; she has practiced the art of "Recollection"; she has looked on the things that are unseen and eternal until they seem the realities of which the things seen and temporal are only the shadows. With all our ministerial need for wider reading, it is nevertheless true that many of us read too much and think too little. And how rare among us is that contemplation in which the creative insights of the mystics and saints are born.[20] With what force comes the chastening word of Fénelon: "How can you expect God to speak in that gentle and inward voice which melts the soul, when you are making so much noise with your rapid reflections? Be silent and God will speak again." [21] Mystic contemplation is more than kaleidoscopic reflection, more than hard-strained thinking, more

[19] John 3:8.
[20] For further development of this point see Chapter V.
[21] Fénelon: *Spiritual Letters*, No. XXII.

even than quick meditation. It is the open-eyed and open-hearted confrontation of God objectified. In contemplation the mind is outward bound; in meditation it may be turned in on itself. In contemplation the spirit is "lost in wonder, love and praise"; in meditation it may be straining to find itself. These moods of high contemplation cannot be held steadily; they fluctuate. And then comes the supplementing and sustaining aid of meditation, as sailors turn to the oars when the wind leaves the sails useless.

The prophetic voice emerges from the luminous silence of brooding listeners, where "deep calleth unto deep." In Joubert's description: "These spirits, lovers of light, when they have an idea, brood long over it first and wait patiently until it shines." Our hurrying generation is so devoid of the patience necessary for developing our mental pictures of God's revealing moments. The vaults of divine revelation operate, as it were, by a time lock. In my office is a small safe which can be opened at any time by anyone who knows the combination; but in the bank across the street the great safe opens only when the appointed time has elapsed. Similarly little compensations and communications may come quickly, but the richest values and revelations await the opening of God's time locks. In patience we possess our souls because by patience we possess the Spirit of God.

And while, as we have said, these mystical moods cannot be preached about, they can be communicated to a congregation. We cannot show the footprints of intuition, but we can start others on the stairs which lead to the throne of God. One of our ministerial errors is that we try to induce prayer by citing *examples* rather than by giving *exercises*. Also we stress the need rather than impart the feeling of prayer. To show an anæmic patient the picture of a famine sufferer may convince him that he ought to eat, but the sight of a succulent steak is far more effective in arousing his appetite. We stress the sterility of prayerless living and we recount the amazing examples of answered prayer, but we are not so proficient in helping men to "taste and see that the Lord is good." That comes through exercises, not through the citing of examples.

Mystical insights must of course be safeguarded by social outlooks. Individual confrontation of the Holy Spirit may evaporate without generating any redemptive power. In fact, one may experience the apparent symptoms of inspiration without catching a revelation of God. The orator may have an inspiration but the prophetic preacher must come with a revelation. Have we not seen persons who seemed "possessed," yet they hardly seemed possessed of the Lord. Sometimes a seemingly demonic spirit can take possession of a personality. Thus Paul said about certain of his deeds: "It is no more I that do it, but sin that dwelleth in me." Our periods of possession, our moments of mystic insight must be tested for evidences of divine revelation.

(e) *Through the Church*

And now we turn to those other sources of revelation which serve to test our individual inspirations as well as to sustain them. The best authenticated Christian mystics, such as Evelyn Underhill and Baron von Hügel, stress the importance of the *church* both as a corrective and a quickener of individual insight. Through the church we summon the collective wisdom of the ages to guide and reinforce our fleeting glimpses of eternal truth. In her traditions we have a background which can be limiting but also enlarging. In her doctrines we have the distilled residuum of faith from those laboratories of life wherein our forefathers tested their experiences. In her creeds we have not definitions which should serve as the terminals of our thought but directions which should show the lines for further advance. In her ritual we have the *cultus* which has proved a means of grace to those who sought the mercy seat of God. In her hymnology we have the marching songs which show us where the saints have trod and serve to carry our spirits through the valley of the shadow. In her sacraments we enter into those revelatory events where life leaps through language and escapes. Uncounted Christians could join with Dr. Charles Clayton Morrison in his testimony of indebtedness to the church: "I see through eyes that have been formed by it. My values have been given me by my participation in it. The God Who has revealed Himself in this community commands my supreme devotion. No other community that I know offers me a revelation of God comparable to that which Christ has given me through the community of which He is center and head." [22]

Admitting that the church has too often muzzled the voices of prophets; that, laden with institutional impedimenta, the church has clung to the paved roads of conventional morality instead of cutting across untrodden fields with the daring reformers; that in her parochial and sectarian divisiveness the church has disgraced the body of Christ; that even the new slogan, "Let the church be the church" may carry an ecclesiasticism less inclusive than the Kingdom, and, as recently appears in some of the spokesmen, an authority less commanding than nationalism; nevertheless, it is high time to re-examine and re-emphasize the church as a strand of revelation.

The doctrines of the church carry more than the weight of numbers and the honor of time, for the church qualifies as an expert in things spiritual. More than that, the church

[22] *Christian Century,* March 26, 1941, p. 424.

is the community in which the participant shares in that concern for righteousness and that commitment to righteousness, which we have noted as the prerequisites for apprehending the revelatory event. While we cannot agree with the statement that "there is no 'standard' outside the Christian community for judging the event in revelation," we do recognize the church as the supreme pattern in history which reveals God.

When a preacher ascends his pulpit, he should remember that the church provides him with the sounding board of the centuries. It was said of Dante that he was the voice of ten silent centuries. The spokesman of God should feel himself near to bursting with the pent-up experience of the ages waiting to find voice through him. What dignity of spiritual bearing and what urgency of spiritual witness are given by such a conception of one's calling.

Various Lyman Beecher Lecturers through the years have noted that doctrinal sermons were not popular. Doctrinal labels are no more popular today. But life situations can be so treated that they lead into the great formative doctrines of our faith. And a revived study of the historic doctrines would deliver us from the preacher's subjectivity, his monotony, his digressions and his limitations. Some time ago a woman said to a minister, "Why is it that when I wish to hear what the church teaches I have to tune in on some Roman Catholic or Fundamentalist preacher?" While the question reveals the inquirer's limited acquaintance, it also should arouse us to the lack of solid teaching in so much contemporary Protestant preaching of the liberal type. We have assumed that doctrinal preaching is too heavy for our stream-lining spiritual diet. In our effort to make our services "bright, breezy and brotherly" we forget that light and air without food is too rapidly reducing, that it makes for leanness of soul. Some preachers are like matches in that they carry all their brilliance in their own heads, and their sermons are but little unrelated flashes of cleverness caused by contact with whatever contingency has most recently rubbed against them. In contrast, the great historic doctrines of faith, like the filament of the electric light, serve as the medium of incandescence. When charged with personal feeling they become aglow with a steady light which brings the radiance of the eternal to the reading of the timely.

(f) *Through the Bible*

Individual mystical insight and the collective experience of the church must ever be tested and reinforced by another source of revelation—*the Bible*. Mystics, when unmoored from the historic content of the Christian faith, float off in nebulous speculation becoming "clouds without water, carried about of winds." [23] The church, when it assumed overweening authority as infallible interpreter of God's will, needed a Reformation to restore the relationship of the branches to the vine. Wholesome, therefore, is the Barthian emphasis in so far as it brings us back to the Bible as the Christian's creative and corrective source of revelation.

While it is too late in the day to try to limit the revelation of the living and ever-speaking God to the recorded Hebrew-Christian Scriptures, it is imperative to recall us to their uniqueness and fertilizing power before contemporary Christianity lapses further into sterility. That the Bible has ceased to be the handbook of Christians is not disproved by the fact that it is still the world's best seller, or even by the report that the sale of the Scriptures in Germany during 1939 exceeded that of *Mein Kampf*. In too

[23] Jude 12.

many homes the Bible is kept as a sort of amulet, an unread "good book," cherished in a sentimental, if not superstitious, spirit. Even church "pillars" treat the Bible somewhat as lovelorn maidens are wont to treat wedding cake, that is, they break it in small pieces and sleep on it, a little bit this Sunday, a little portion next Sunday; but as far as any daily feeding on it as the bread of life, how few are they that do it. The pulpit, realizing that the Bible is not popular with the pew, tends to avoid the dry fields of scripture to range widely over the most recent secular writings. Religious education seems to share the popular aversion to Biblical study and tries to catch the young minds with up-to-the-minute projects designed to inculcate ethical principles but often devoid of reference to historic religion. Moreover, religious education is regarded by most church members as something which is supposed to stop at the teen age. Thus, the prevailing attitude toward the Bible even in church precincts is somewhat parallel to that of the college sophomore toward astronomy. Finding herself seated beside a stranger at dinner, she asked what he did. He replied that he taught astronomy. "How interesting!" she exclaimed. "We finished that last semester." The Bible, the source book of the renewing Gospel, is regarded by the majority of Christians as something they finished in Sunday School. Thus has developed a generation of scriptural illiterates. And it is an open question whether Protestantism with all its boast of bringing the Bible to the individual's enlightenment is doing as thorough a job of teaching the book as is done by Roman Catholicism.

The word of God is in the Bible as the spirit is in the body, but the Scriptures are not a doctrinal protocol. When we think of the Bible as a body of statement, it becomes an object of study. When we view it as a description of the ways by which divine revelation is received, it becomes a means of study. While the Bible is both an object and a means of study, it is the latter which needs emphasizing. Instead of spending so much time searching for keys to the Scriptures, we do better to use the Scriptures as the keys for unlocking the secrets of progressive revelation. We should look *with* the seers rather than *at* them.

Portions of the Bible are external history, written by spectators and hence subject to study and interpretation as case history. But other parts are "inner history" and can only be apprehended by participation. Thus when we delve into the book of Deuteronomy, we read of codes which are objects of historic interest, adapted to a certain stage of social development. And then in their midst we come upon a line like this: "The eternal God is thy refuge and underneath are the everlasting arms." [24] In the spirit of Browning's "We musicians know," we can say to a statement like that, "We sufferers know." Those who have lived deeply do not need to argue whether the author of such words had found a voice not his own. Such words find us. We may be puzzled by the parallel accounts of creation as given in Genesis, but when we enter beneath the symbolism of the Eden account we are no longer disturbed about questions of geology and evolution for we realize that the geography of that garden is the universal human heart and the date of that fall is yesterday, today and forever. Passages of "external history" can be committed to memory; but passages of "inner history" can be grasped only by committing them to life. In using the Bible as a source of revelation, we must desire to *be* something, not merely to *know* something.

When we abide in the moods of the Biblical writers until

[24] Deuteronomy 3:27.

their words abide in us, then are we truly their disciples, able to catch the flash of their inspiration. Then "deep calleth unto deep." Then we listen to psalms whose haunting beauty and truth linger so timelessly on the air of the ages that we feel sure the authors were thinking God's thoughts after him. We hear prophets moving so far ahead of their contemporaries that we cannot explain their words as the echoes of the crowd but as the voice of the Eternal. When critics say that what men call the voice of God is only the projection of their own wish-thinking, the words of the prophets rise to refute such charges, for they felt themselves confronted by a God who was anything but comfortable. Wishful thinking may call for a God to die *with*, but the prophets heard the call of a God to die *for*. The probing force and searching insistence of the Hebrew prophets—whence came they if not from God? Those words which stir us to creative effort and new capacity for goodness, which know no limits of date or region but continue age after age in all lands to speak to men as though out of eternity—what are these words if not revelation of the divine?

After James Russell Lowell heard Emerson deliver the Phi Beta Kappa address at Harvard in 1867, he wrote: "Emerson's oration . . . began nowhere and ended everywhere and yet as always with that divine man, it left you feeling that something beautiful had passed that way— something more beautiful than anything else, like the rising and setting of the stars." Perhaps it is some such impression that the general reader gets from his reading of those favorite passages which commonly constitute his contact with the Bible. They are luminous like stars but seemingly unrelated. Speaking for myself, I find God speaking even more clearly in the sequence of His unfolding revelation

than in the flashes of individual inspiration. When I follow
a people dug out of obscurity in the dim misty morning of
the patriarchs, tested in hardships of Egyptian slavery,
welded into a nation by Saul and David, broken into bits
by the sons of Solomon, scattered in the adversities of exile
yet held together by a deathless hope, until in the fullness
of time One appeared who proves the key for interpreting
all that preceded him—for all this I have no better explanation than that given by the Epistle to the Hebrews: "God
who at sundry times and in divers manners spake in times
past unto the fathers by the prophets, hath in these last
days spoken unto us by his Son." [25]

From the birth of conscience in Eden to the birth of a
nation in Jerusalem to the birth of a Savior in Bethlehem
to the birth of a church at Pentecost—so runs the divine
drama of redemption. Thus on the horizon of history is
limned the long upward striving of the human spirit. The
generations are linked together by faith. The old men
dream their dreams and the young men catch their visions
and carry on their ideals toward further goals. And out of
all the disappointments and delays, the sins and setbacks
of history, the divine purpose is portrayed as a kind of relay
race run by those who are "looking unto Jesus the author
and finisher of our faith." [26] If it be said of these followers
of faith, "God is not ashamed to be called their God," [27]
then I am not ashamed to confess my faith that this upward
striving of the race is the leading of a living God. Those
who warn us to look for the depravity of man rather than
his divinity deepen my sense of the divine leading but they
do not lessen my sense of human dignity. "Know ye not

[25] Hebrews 1:1, 2.
[26] *Ibid.*, 12:2.
[27] *Ibid.*, 11:16.

that ye are the temple of God, and that the spirit of God dwelleth in you?" [28]

(g) *Through the Author and Finisher of Our Faith*

And now we too look unto him who is "the author and finisher of our faith" in the God who speaks. In Jesus Christ we have the Word made flesh. In him we have the Word which illumines all lesser revelations of God. The glimpses we get of God in the faces of His seekers and finders, in the fidelities of nature, in the luminous moments of inspiration, in the beloved community of the church, in the enduring and unfolding insights of Scripture—all these find their fulfillment, aye and their foundation, in Christ. "He is before all things and by him all things consist." [29]

"Man," says John Middleton Murry, "cannot accept certainties; he must discover them. No matter how beautifully, how profoundly, how finally Christ formulated the everlasting truths of religion, in order to know that they are everlasting, in order to know simply what they mean, man must rediscover them in himself." [30] And that is precisely the platform on which Christ made his plea for recognition as the revealer of God. To the disciples of John who followed him, inquiring where he dwelt, his reply was, "Come and see." It was the invitation to life's laboratory. The Fourth Gospel correctly interprets the spirit of the Christ throughout when it reports him saying: "My doctrine is not mine, but his that sent me. If any man will do his will, he shall know of the doctrine, whether it be of God or whether I speak of myself." [31] Jesus adhered to the pragmatic test. His authority is one that commands because

[28] I Corinthians 3:16.
[29] Colossians 1:17.
[30] J. Middleton Murry: "Literature and Religion" in *The Necessity of Art* edited by A. Clutton-Brock, London, p. 161.
[31] John 7:17.

it also creates the power to interpret his teaching through a moral and religious consciousness. His authority is sustained by the fact that he does not ask his disciples to take his word for the truth of what he utters. He leaves us free in mind, but as we listen to his words and live in the presence of his personality we become conscious of a compelling imperative. Like all true authority which one personality exerts upon another, it is not imposed as external and infallible. It imposes itself. "We need no other credential than Christ himself. The basis of Christ's authority is not a prior belief in his divinity or his miracles, but the impression which his Personality makes on us." [32]

And the personality of Christ is one feature of our faith about which there is no lingering uncertainty. The synoptic Gospels, viewing the historic Jesus from differing angles of interest, and the Fourth Gospel, interpreting the Christ of faith—all unite to give a composite portrait of a personality consistent throughout. However we may differ as to dates and details of his career, his character is too clear for controversy. Under the spotlight of criticism, men have not "seen through" Christ to any false elements of character, but the longer they have looked the more they "behold the glory of God in the face of Jesus Christ."

It is this self-authenticating interpretation and this self-imparting personality of Christ which make him the "author" as well as the "finisher" of our faith in the God who speaks. The lower levels of revelation do not lead us up to Christ. Rather, it is Christ who leads us to find the revelation of the living God on the lower levels which we have mentioned in this chapter.

Take any one of them. True, as we have said, we find

[32] R. H. Strachan: *The Authority of Christian Experience*, Cokesbury Press, p. 199.

God revealed in those who are searching for Him. But if our own sight were wholly unillumined by the outlook of Christ, we might look at the lookers and see only, as did a traveler in Europe after the World War, a stupid unseeing faith resembling that of blindfolded camels treading the rounds of an Egyptian waterwheel deceived in the darkness with the thought that they were going to illimitable distances. When, however, we try "to let that mind be in us which was in Christ Jesus," our vision is sharpened by the realistic insight of love which is far more deeply penetrating than the skepticism on which men pride themselves. We get those glimpses into the heart of human nature which are "hidden from the wise and prudent" and revealed unto the childlike and innocent who open themselves wholeheartedly to the goodness which they see. With the mind of Christ we observe the cheap theatricality and tawdry jewelry with which man struts upon his little stage, but we also see the heavenly plot which haunts man's mind and the divine drama which haltingly he tries to play. With the insight of Christlike love we see the depravity of man's fallen nature but also the grace after which he is groping, and what is more, the divine grace which keeps its grip on man. Thus Christ causes us to hear the God who speaks amid the mutterings of our maddened humanity.

> Where cross the crowded ways of life,
> Where sound the cries of race and clan,
> Above the voice of selfish strife,
> We hear thy voice, O Son of Man.[33]

Or turn to another of the above-mentioned places of God's revealing, namely, that of nature. While the fidelities and grace of natural creation may serve as altar stairs

[33] Frank Mason North, *Hymn*.

to God's broadcasting chamber, the surer ascent is *with* Christ rather than *to* Christ. Aesthetic stimulation through sunsets and mountain vistas may end far short of mystic contemplation or the sustaining sense of God's comradeship. The immensity and orderliness of creation may overwhelm us with awe of a divinity too distant for companionship. "When I consider thy heavens, the work of thy fingers, the moon and the stars which thou hast ordained: what is man that thou art mindful of him?" [34] Or we may see nature "red in tooth and claw." No, we cannot trust Mother Nature to lead us to the Father of our Lord Jesus Christ. But when we turn to nature with that mind which was in Christ, then the realization steals over us that the greatest thing in all creation is personality. The power of Niagara, the size of a planetary system, the force of the sun itself, none of these can equal the mysterious grandeur of personality, with its ability to think, to value, to love and to hope. And if personality is the highest form of creation, and if Jesus of Nazareth is the highest expression of personality we have seen or can imagine, then in his personality we see the image of the Divine Creator, for God to be God must be the highest we can conceive. When we first look at Christ long enough to learn his method and measure of interpretation, then this physical universe, with all its illimitable vastness and its inexplicable cruelties, speaks with a Galilean accent.

In Christ we see revealed the purpose for which "the whole creation groaneth and travaileth in pain together until now." [35] He conveys the conviction that this earth with all its vicissitudes and retrogressions is not a meaningless vale of tears, but "a vale of soul-making" in the control

[34] Psalms 8:3, 4.
[35] Romans 8:22.

of a Heavenly Father whose purpose is the rearing of sons into fullness of life. In Christ we see God's "design for living."

To use Christ thus as the interpreter of nature's revelation may seem to some an unrealistic coloring of the observer's lens. To be sure, the Christian does view nature in technicolor. But the meaning-maker's observations are always colored by his inner concepts, his "apperception mass." Coleridge expressed this truth when sojourning in the Harz Forest:

> . . . For I had found
> That outward forms, the loftiest, still receive
> Their finer influence from the Life within;
> Fair cyphers else: fair, but of import vague
> Or unconcerning." [36]

The Christian frankly admits that his view of the external world is colored by the mind of Christ, but he maintains that thereby he catches the true colors of creation's handiwork. To look with Christ is to view not through the roseate tints of idealization but through the ripened experience of life. The veteran viewer who saw in Christ the revelation of the divine event toward which the whole creation moves tells us the stages through which he took his observations: "Tribulation worketh patience; and patience, experience; and experience, hope: and hope maketh not ashamed." [37] Those who would seemingly have most reason to doubt the goodness of God—it is they who are most convinced of his Christlikeness. Along the streams of life as on the banks of the Jordan, "Come and see" is the invitation which Christ confidently extends to those who would know whether he is the revealer of God.

[36] S. T. Coleridge: "Lines Written at Elbingerode," lines 16–20.
[37] Romans 5:3, 4.

Or turn with Christ to those inner illuminating experiences, which we have mentioned as another place where
God speaks to us. When we sit down to hold converse with
the Man of Nazareth, we rise like the woman of Samaria to
cry, "Come, see a man which told me all things that ever I
did: is not this the Christ?" [38] He uncovers our buried
selves. He sets us rummaging among our memories. He re-
opens within us the wells of living water. He shows us the
persons we were meant to be, aye, and the persons we still
can be. He reveals the God who worketh in us. However
hardened we may have become by the world's artifices and
cruelties, we feel ourselves coming back to our real natures
in the presence of the Galilean.

Bethlehem is the place where the best in us comes to
birth. And Calvary is the hill where the highest in us feels
holy kinship. Something within us rises to recognize that
in the cross love, the holiest thing in life, spoke its last
word. There we see One who died not merely in loyalty
to a cause, as a scientist might give his life in a laboratory
for the furtherance of truth. There we see a Christ, who
died not merely in loyalty to a nation or a party, as a soldier
perishes in battle. Christ died in redeeming love that he
might bring to God all men out of every kindred and
tongue and people and nation. "Greater love hath no man
than this, that a man lay down his life for his friends." [39]
But this must be read in the light of Calvary's scope, and
then we see that no other man had love like unto Christ,
for no other gave such all-inclusive definition of friendship.
The dimensions of Christ's love convince us of its divinity.
When we are "able to comprehend with all saints what is
the breadth, and length, and depth, and height and know

[38] John 4:29.
[39] John 15:13.

the love of Christ," [40] then we reach the conclusion that "God was in Christ reconciling the world unto himself." [41] In his words we hear the God who speaks.[42]

4. *The Listener Speaks*

The man who is sensitive enough to receive the revelation of God is likely to be smitten at first with a reticent reverence. Like the young Jeremiah, he cries, "Oh, Lord God! Behold, I cannot speak: for I am a child." [43] The person who is worthy to be a prophet feels loath to assume the function. The propagandist may rush into print, but the prophet of God does not rush into the preaching office. Convinced though he is that the Word of God has come to him, he is restrained by the sense of his inadequacy as an interpreter, his unworthiness as an exemplar, his fallibility as a formulator of specific applications. It seems so presumptuous to stand in public as the spokesmen of God when we confront conditions so complex that we are baffled to define concretely the course of the divine will.

Impelled by the divine imperative to proclaim the word, yet restrained by an integrity which hesitates to declare

[40] Ephesians 3:18-19.
[41] II Corinthians 5:19.
[42] Recently I have had occasion to observe the methods of the veteran missionary, Dr. Frank Laubach. Much has been written about "practicing the presence of God"; but he is stressing the practice of the presence of Christ. Laubach believes, and rightly I think, that most of us need a mental picture to make God's presence vividly real. In his "Game of Minutes" he cultivates the habit of visualizing and vocalizing Christ as frequently as possible. He not only talks to Christ but he tries to phrase what Christ would say to him in hourly situations. Some may not need such devotional aids, and to some such techniques may seem too anthropomorphic. But if we are to hear the God who speaks, we must visualize a Personality to whom we speak.
[43] Jeremiah 1:6.

more than he knows, the prophet is in danger of narrowing the range of his pronouncements. He knows what is wrong; he does not so clearly see the concrete ways of setting it right. Therefore his tendency is to specialize on denunciation and attack. Thus the term "prophet" conjures up in the lay mind the figure of the flaming crusader, the scathing accuser, the stern stalker of the guilty, the flayer of public corruption. Elijah, Amos, John the Baptist, Savonarola—such are the prophet patterns. Courage is the hallmark of the prophet's calling and the sword of the spirit is the symbol of his office. When preachers or sermons possess these austere characteristics, the public accords the label, "prophetic."

To be sure, courage is a *sine qua non* of God's spokesman. And when we think of the entrenched evils to be attacked, it seems a bit soft to speak of a winsome prophet. And sickening indeed is the spineless compromising preaching all too common. But when did courage become inconsistent with winsomeness? To reveal God is the central and essential function of the prophet; and the God to be revealed is "the Father of our Lord Jesus Christ, the Father of mercies, and the God of all comfort." [44] Did not the rugged Elijah have a mountain experience which taught him that after the wind and lightning and earthquake God spoke in the still small voice? Is Isaiah's prophetic courage made soft by the inclusion of the revelation, "Comfort ye, comfort ye my people, saith your God"? [45] In fact that is the preface which John the Baptist took to himself when he became "the voice of him that crieth in the wilderness, Prepare ye the way of the Lord." To comfort through courage rather than by coddling is the prophet's function.

[44] II Corinthians 1:3.
[45] Isaiah 40:1.

To hearten the good by the infusion of spiritual strength is as much his task as to hammer at the evil.

Not to mute the diapason notes of stern denunciation, but to balance them with the full gamut of divine love is the rôle of him who would reveal God. Some time ago a minister found himself unacceptable to his parish and was forced to resign. The man was conscientious and courageous. He had attacked certain social evils. The impression went abroad that he had been crucified for his courage. No doubt such a conclusion was largely justified. But one of the parish officials in defending the laymen made a significant point when he said through the press that the trouble lay not so much in what the minister talked about as in what he did not preach. The situation was that the preacher's social passion had invited some criticism. Thereupon he developed a martyr complex. He felt called to keep striking the same chord. He neglected the notes of comfort, of encouragement, of prayer. No congregation can stand continuous harping on the same string—and no string, however good, can stand it.

Prophetic courage is not lessened but made effective by keeping the message comprehensive. Consider the inclusiveness of the prophetic office as announced through Zacharias, the Baptist's father: "And thou, child, shalt be called the prophet of the Highest: for thou shalt go before the face of the Lord to prepare his ways: to give knowledge of salvation to his people by the remission of their sins, through the tender mercy of our God; whereby the dayspring from on high hath visited us, to give light to them that sit in darkness and in the shadow of death, to guide our feet into the way of peace." [46] In preparing the way of the Lord, there must be some blasting; in opening hard hearts there

[46] Luke 1:76–79.

must be some hammering. But the trouble with our living is that it is fragmentary as well as fractious. To hammer, therefore, is not enough, for hammering only serves to break into still smaller fragments. It is the power to put together which we need pre-eminently. The man who can analyze and not synthesize becomes a man of shreds and fragments, like Shakespeare's pedant who had been at a feast of languages and stolen all the scraps.

This comprehensiveness of the prophet's commission gives a *seer-like quality* to his outlook. The terms "to prophesy" and "to predict" have been used confusingly. The great Hebrew prophets stood forth in distinction from the schools of professional "prophets" who played the rôle of soothsayers. The spurious art of divination was discarded by the Scriptural prophets who strove to convey the will of God rather than to cater to the wishes of men. And we repeatedly re-emphasize that the prophet's function is to forth-tell and not to foretell. Nevertheless, the prophet does have a legitimate power of prediction by the very comprehensiveness of his outlook. He sees the "pattern shown in the mount" which lures man with its vision, however far he wanders in his vice. He senses the recurring rhythms of life's flow. He keeps ever before him that wholeness toward which the holy and healing God tends to restore our fragmentary living. Thus Jeremiah announces, "I see a rod of an almond tree." [47] The budding almond, the first harbinger of spring, was visible to the prophet who saw the stirring of God's springtime during the depths of Israel's spiritual winter. No magic crystal gazer he; but one who saw with crystalline clearness the fidelities of God on which the future rests. By keeping close to God, the prophet is ahead of the crowd's calendar.

[47] Jeremiah 1:11.

With a courage sufficiently comprehensive to give comfort and vision, the prophet is *creative* in his total impact. He cuts out the cancerous evil, but with a healing surgery. He clears the ground, but by methods designed to make it a garden. Like Jeremiah's, his commission is conceived as ultimately constructive: "I have this day set thee over the nations and over the kingdoms, to root out, and to pull down, and to destroy, and to throw down, to *build* and to plant." [48] The propagandist or social reformer may have his eye on the ills to be removed: the prophet considers also the means of their removal, for he knows that the means serve to shape the ends. Thus the prophet of God sees the fallacy of wars to end war, of trying to drive out dictators with methods that destroy the seeds of democracy. He lays the axe at the root of barren institutions which have cumbered the ground long enough; but he is so sensitive to any lingering signs of life that he pleads for extra time till he "dig about it and dung it; and if it bear fruit, well; and if not, then after that thou shalt cut it down." [49] The prophet carries a spade as well as an axe, for he sees his mission as that of making virtue grow—a more difficult task than merely cutting out vice. He is a creator rather than a critic.

In short, the prophet of God who speaks in the name of Christ can do no less than take to himself the inclusive and constructive commission which Jesus took over from Isaiah's prophecy: "The Spirit of the Lord is upon me, because he hath anointed me to preach the gospel to the poor; he hath sent me to heal the broken-hearted, to preach deliverance to the captives, and recovering of sight to the blind, to set at liberty them that are bruised, to preach the accept-

[48] Jeremiah 1:10.
[49] Luke 13:9.

able year of the Lord." [50] If any brave young prophet thinks such work will dull the fighting edge of his social crusades, let him try it. Every one of the above functions runs straight into a fight. The point is to make the fight eventuate in the peace of God.

[50] Luke 4:18–19.

Chapter IV

MORE THAN A PROPHET

But what went ye out for to see? A prophet? Yea, I say unto you, and much more than a prophet. This is he, of whom it is written, Behold, I send my messenger before thy face, which shall prepare thy way before thee.

LUKE 7:26, 27.

. . . the fire of God
Fills him. I never saw his like; there lives
No greater leader.
ALFRED, LORD TENNYSON, *Lancelot and Elaine*, lines 314–316.

Chapter IV

MORE THAN A PROPHET

1. *The Primacy of Personality*

Our wilderness is so full of voices that where words multiply their weight is divided. Henry Ward Beecher took note in his day of the shadow which the press was throwing on the prestige of the pulpit. He remarked that, whereas the preacher spoke to his people only once a week, the daily press reached them seven times during the same period. Now our enterprising dailies offer as many as seven editions in one day; and the radio furnishes its hearers with daily opinion-formers some seventy times seven. Amid such a surfeit of voices, the prophet finds it ever more difficult to win a hearing.

Furthermore, the prevalence of propaganda has made minds increasingly deaf to direct appeal. The per capita cost of conversion through preaching is increasing. But at the same time, it would seem that as men steel themselves against direct appeal they are becoming more susceptible to indirect influence. Never did fashion and "atmosphere" seem more pervasive and potent than now. Style-setting in mental and moral attitudes is as rapid and subtle as in manners and dress. In the realm of religion this means that the power of personality increases as the force of direct appeal diminishes. We may frankly admit that the word "preaching" has an unpopular connotation. The word suggests a form of propaganda, an effort to put something over, to make others "be good."

Some years ago the writer was at a New England college on the Sunday following the matriculation address of a new president. The applause for that address was still echoing on the campus. In his remarks the president had said that he did not wish to preach to them, that he himself did not like a lot of rules, but that there were certain conventions which gentlemen everywhere observe. Those conventions, he said, would be respected on that campus. Why did the students like that message? Because the president seemed to them to be setting a style of conduct without much apparent effort to preach it down at them. And in that attitude the president was approximating the method of Jesus. Our Lord did not dash up and down Palestine like a propagandist, trying to put across a program. He had time to stop and play with little children, to sit and talk with despairing souls beside Samaritan wells. When they brought to him a woman taken in adultery, it might have seemed a strategic occasion to deliver a sermon on sin. But Jesus did not count on words to carry his point. With a gentleman's reserve he did not even look at the woman to add to her confusion. He stooped and wrote in the sand. Then when she and her accusers had had time to regain a thinking posture, he said, "He that is without sin among you, let him first cast a stone at her." [1] The propagandist, yes, even the prophet, would have been concerned primarily to assert the moral order, but Jesus aimed at the saving of a personality. The Magdalene was an end in herself, not a means to an end. Since his aim was to reach and redeem persons, his most effective means was through personality. He was the incarnate Word.

Despite the depersonalizing influence of mechanical means of communication, the personality behind the words

[1] John 8:7.

is becoming ever more important. Not what is said, but who says it—that is the consideration which gives weight to what we hear. When we open a magazine, we read the "who's who" in order to appraise the articles. In view of this, there need be no fear that radio preaching will replace the pastor-preacher. Nor is it feasible to think, as has sometimes been suggested, that with tomorrow's increasing specialization, we can count on traveling schools of prophets from theological seminaries or elsewhere to furnish the sermons while the minister of the parish confines himself to the management of its multiform activities. Men will be most responsive to the minister whom they know. They will follow a trusted leader even into untried mental territory. The first hope of winning men to new viewpoints lies in those pastors who have gained their personal confidence. The preacher must be more than a voice, more than a prophet.

Consider the life of Henry Drummond, who was pastor to a passing throng. Few men have been more mastered by a central purpose. He lived to bring men into fellowship with Jesus Christ, and the influence of his preaching and his personal interviews upon the student life of Scotland lived long after he was gone. His biographer [2] says that writing the story of his life is "like writing the history of a fragrance." The buoyancy of his daily life may be seen from the following excerpt: "You found him keen for any of a hundred interests. He fished, he shot, he skated as few can, he played cricket; he would go any distance to see a fire or football match. He had a new story, a new puzzle, or a new joke every time he met you. If it was a rainy afternoon in a country house, he described a new game, and in five

[2] George Adam Smith: *Life of Henry Drummond*, McClure, Phillips & Co., p. 13.

minutes everybody was playing it. If it was a children's party, they clamored for his sleight of hand. . . . The name he went by among younger men was 'The Prince.' There was a distinction and a radiance upon him that compelled the title." [3] The response to such a personality is expressed by one of Shakespeare's nobles to King Lear, "You have that in your countenance which I would fain call master." [4]

2. *Forerunner As Well As Follower*

In preparing the way for his message, the minister plays a two-fold rôle. In the fortieth chapter of Isaiah is found the command which the Baptist took to himself. "Prepare ye the way of the Lord." In the sixty-second chapter of the same prophecy comes another call, "Prepare ye the way of the people." Put the two commands together and we have the double duty of the Lord's ambassador. He is guide in a two-fold search. On the one side is God, longing for His lost children, brooding over their waywardness, seeking a way to reach their unreconciled hearts. On the other side are men, restlessly searching for something beyond themselves, gnawed by a hunger deeper than physical, homesick in their homes. The preacher's task is to bring the longing Heavenly Father and His seeking bewildered children together.

The minister is thus both a follower of the Lord and also a forerunner of the Lord. As a guide to God he prepares a way for the people to come after him. As a forerunner of the Lord he prepares a way by which the divine influence follows his own footsteps. Since God is both immanent and

[3] *Idem,* pp. 2–3.
[4] *King Lear,* I, 4, 28.

transcendent, the one in "whom we live and move and have
our being," we can hardly separate functionally the work
of preparing the way of the Lord from the work of preparing the way of the people. When Phillips Brooks preached
from Trinity pulpit he was projecting the way of the Lord
into the wilderness of men's bewildered minds, and when
he walked through the streets of Boston his radiant personality made more luminous the road by which men could
reach their Lord. Yet it might equally well be said that his
words opened the way of the people to the Lord, and his
walk opened the way of the Lord to his people. After Ian
Maclaren left his parish, his successor said that the most
verdant memories of his ministry were not of his uniquely
interesting sermons but of the stories he told to sick little
children as he sat beside their crumby beds and brought
smiles to their feverish faces. Preaching and personality are
inextricably intertwined.

In this double search, however, the roadmaker may distinguish two aspects of his task, that of preparing the people
for the word, and that of preparing the word for the people.
Let us consider the first, for in practice it must precede the
second. To say that a minister should prepare his people
before his message is somewhat more than to say that pastoral work is the way to open unresponsive hearts. A pastor
may win the affections of a parish so that his word is welcomed, and yet he may not be making a way for the Lord.
He may draw a crowd without drawing the Divine Presence. His efforts may end with his egocentric efficiency.
He may be personally magnetic without being spiritually
dynamic.

The success of a preacher is commonly gauged by his
popular following; but the power of the preacher is measured by his divine following. When he enters a situation

does he make a way for the Lord to follow him? Is he a forerunner of One greater than himself "the latchet of whose shoes" he is "not worthy to unloose"? Is his the Baptist's spirit which says, "He must increase, but I must decrease"? [5] When his shadow falls athwart a threshold, do men see the Light behind him? When he speaks, do listeners hear the Word beyond his words?

Let us turn this searching test to a few situations which confront the Lord's roadmakers. Around us are bewildered men. Not merely are they unable to find the familiar landmarks because of the world's foggy weather, but they have lost their sense of moral direction. They are caught in the confusion of their own compromises. As we move among them, do we have a way with us that shows we know the way to the Father? Do those who watch us get a more vivid sense of divine guidance? Although we may not be able to give definitive solutions to their complex problems, do we have a simple directness of motive which helps toward the taking of the next steps and the doing of the nearest duties? If so, then we are fulfilling the commission, "Prepare ye the way of the Lord, make his paths straight."

Around us are men depressed in mood because of their individual situations or because of the world's tragedies. They are going through the valley of the shadow where the twilight comes too soon. Do we disturb such persons with the joy of elevated thoughts? To lift others out of their low moods, to lead them to the rock that is higher than we, where their eyes sweep the far horizons, to leave them looking up—that is to "prepare the way of the Lord."

Another question, Do we arouse others to a sense of earnest purpose? Around us are those who are frittering away their energies in trivialities, perhaps in frivolities.

[5] John 3:30.

They live a butterfly existence if they are prospero[...]
perhaps they live a grub-worm existence if they are p[...]
What is our effect on such persons? To impress them w[...]
the dignity of life, to impart a worthwhile purpose wh[...]
life has become pointless, to put flavor back into living
when life has become stale, flat and unprofitable—that is
to "prepare the way of the Lord."

Another question. Do we soften hearts that are hard?
Around us are persons who have become callous through
the world's rough handling, or even embittered by brutal
circumstances. Does our association with such people soften
or stir their resentments? Does our conversation confirm or
remove their prejudices? To bring balm to minds that are
bruised, to sweeten lives that have become sour, to quicken
the reconciling spirit which sends them out to forgive and
be forgiven, to kindle the warmth of kindly feeling in cold
hearts—this is to "prepare the way of the Lord."

Another question. Do we make people forget themselves? When we come into the presence of others, do we
make them self-conscious? Or do we so forget ourselves
that they forget themselves and together we enter into the
fellowship of something greater? Le Grand Cannon, in a
book of fiction which is true to fact, tells of an old evangelist who took as an apprentice a young minister fresh from
theological seminary. The older preacher had his faults,
and one day he asked his young colleague to give his frank
criticism. After the youthful preacher had analyzed the
older man's weaknesses, he in turn asked the experienced
evangelist to take him apart and tell him his faults. He
wanted to know why it was that the older preacher with
all his defects could hold the crowds while he failed to grip
his hearers. The old veteran then told the young fellow that
he was too conscious of himself, of the impressions he was

making. He said: "Forget about yourself. What you want to do is to think about those people. Then maybe you can make them forget about themselves. That's what they've come for. When you can give it to 'em, you'll be a preacher." [6] To think about others until they forget about themselves, to put ourselves in others' shoes until they try to put themselves in ours, thus begetting mutual understanding and sympathy—that is to "prepare the way of the Lord."

Another simple question. Do we restore to persons that self-respect which is the necessary preface to personal salvation and social redemption? Beaten spirits are found in pent-houses as well as in slums, in universities as well as in homes and offices. Men are beaten in spirit by the vastness of the physical universe until they think of it as a pitiless machine without divine origin, meaning or purpose. Men are beaten by adversity until they are seared at the very center of their lives! Men are beaten in spirit by sin, and like a dog returning to lick the hand that flogged it, they come back again and again to the transgressions that are their ruin. Men are beaten in spirit by hopelessness until they look out on human society with no enthusiasm for any worthwhile cause and with no expectation of any betterment. To lift the bruised reed without breaking, to cup the smoldering flax of hope until it flames again, to give men a fresh grip on old verities, to make those who have sinned away their early innocence believe again in the possibility of goodness—this is to "prepare the way of the Lord."

One more searching question. Do we carry a contagious courage which makes others more willing to trust the "Power not ourselves that makes for righteousness"? In a hostile world which crucifies Christ's ideals and ridicules

[6] Le Grand Cannon, Jr.: *A Mighty Fortress*, Farrar & Rinehart, p. 61.

the Christian methods for re-establishing them, do we manifest an apostolic boldness which causes men to take notice that we have been with Jesus? To break the spell of fear-gripped men with the gaiety of godly courage; to stand against social wrong with such invincible faith that others behold us, "enduring as seeing Him who is invisible," then look for the secret of our strength; to be natural and yet suggest the supernatural, to face life with a smile that makes others take heart and then to face death with a courage that keeps others from losing heart—that is to "prepare the way of the Lord."

A national religious weekly has recently run a significant series of articles on the theme, "How my mind has changed in the last ten years." It might be quite as fruitful to run a series on the question, "How my congregation has changed in the last ten years." By this we do not mean the shift of residence and the transiency of personnel, but the improvement of insight, the growth of tolerance, the advance to new viewpoints, the deepening of conviction. Important as it is to know the distance which the mind of the messenger has moved in a decade, it is much more important to know how far his hearers have been moved by his messages. And this cannot be gauged by any Gallup poll taken by circular letters or by any parish votes on which sermons are desired for re-preaching. It can be measured only by a sensitive shepherding personality moving among his people, watching their indirect reactions, their social responses, their off-guard moments.

It is a soul-searching responsibility to be in spiritual charge of a congregation for ten or twenty years. The public has almost unanimously repudiated the "sit-down strike" on the ground that it is unjustifiable to occupy the premises of another and limit its productive use. The principle, when brought home to the pulpit, is a disturbing one. The preacher occupies not only a place which another man might occupy, but also a place which the Holy Spirit is supposed to fill. His workshop is the house of God. Are we who occupy pulpits using the spiritual property of our people to more than a fraction of capacity? Could some other pastor make so much more of our position? Is our leadership limiting the Lord's production? Such questions can be answered only in the secret places of the soul by a minister who hears both calls, "Prepare ye the way of the Lord," and "Prepare ye the way of the people."

3. *Preaching to Life Situations*

The Lord's roadmaker who watches and works for openings into the hearts of his people will naturally find that concern conditioning his messages. He will prepare his sermons with the needs of his people in mind. He will visualize individuals whose secret cares have been revealed to him. His messages will grow out of life situations. He will preach to problems yet not as "problems." His will not be the third-personal mood of a surgeon lecturing to his students over the anæsthetized "case" used for demonstration, but the direct first and second person discussion of a doctor desirous of helping the patient to whom he is speaking. He will speak to real situations and out of actual experience. Starting where people live, he will be sure of their interest at the very beginning; but he thereby assumes a high responsibility, for unless he arrives somewhere he will be equally sure of the listeners' disappointment, if not disgust, at the end. Preaching to life situations is the most fruitful form of sermonizing but it requires the deepest roots. The one who does it must have the people not only in his mind but on his heart. The themes must be secured from quests and not from questionnaires. The sermons must be written not merely in ink but in blood.

"Life-situation preaching" strikes a responsive chord in clergy and people because of its realism. It confronts not theories but conditions. Let us then keep it realistic. If there is one abominable practice to be abhorred, it is that of manufacturing cases to fit the problem and then passing off these pulpit manikins as flesh-and-blood personalities. It is all very well to draw on the imagination for supposed situations as illustrations of a principle, provided we so label them. But to use imaginary cases as actual experience or to enlarge and embellish incidents out of all resemblance to original fact is intellectually dishonest and spiritually perilous. A visiting bishop pictured a case of need with such eloquence and realism that a member of the congregation was moved to come up after the service with an offer of help. The layman asked for the address of the needy one. He was disillusioned and disgusted when he learned that the poor victim existed only in the speaker's imagination. After hearing a well-known preacher of the evangelistic type stir the emotions of a congregation with striking incidents of his pastoral success in saving lost souls, a keen young business woman went to another minister with the question, "Honestly now, do you preachers have all those dramatic experiences you talk about?" One mind at least saw through the homiletical embroidery. If we are trying to make our preaching true to life, let us keep it as true as life.

Life-situation preaching need not be limited to the minister's own experience. The range of reality can be extended through reading, especially the reading of biography. Illustrations from the lives of historical personalities are far more arresting and convincing than analogies, however clever. But let us be very careful about the historicity of our biographical material. And let us not in Emil Ludwig fashion take liberties with the minds of celebrities by reading plausible motives into their actions. Integrity is as truly a Christian virtue as is piety. Many a thoughtful listener has lost confidence in a preacher's reliability because of slovenly inaccuracies in literary or biographical allusions. Homiletic hell is paved with apt but untrue illustrations.

Another warning signal should be noted in preaching to life situations. There is danger of tending too much toward the introspective and self-centered. Dr. Harold Ruopp, who has rendered such valuable service through his analysis of this preaching form,[7] collected the expressions of interest from some four thousand church attendants. His classification of their concerns is revealing and significant. The problems dealing with "the individual and his inner self" constituted 48.7 per cent of the total expressions. These included personality problems, such as the feeling of futility, disharmony, frustration, insecurity, fear, anxiety, loss of a sense of significance; life decisions about education, vocation, marriage, personal moral problems, arising from jealousy, hatred, greed, anger, sex, alcoholism, misfortune, with the questions growing out of accidents, sickness, suicide, death. A second group of problems having to do with "the individual in his relationship to the family" accounted for 21.2 per cent of the responses. The third set of questions, numbering 16.7 per cent of the total, dealt with "the individual in his relationship to larger social groups and society," involving problems of "social inequality, unemployment, the profit motive, Christian citizenship, internationalism and conflicting loyalties." The fourth classifica-

[7] Cf. *The Christian Century Pulpit*, May and June, 1941.

tion, only 13.4 per cent, dealt with "the individual in his relationship to God and the universe," consisting of such issues as the meaning of religion, what is involved in following Jesus, the conflict between science and religion.

On the basis of Doctor Ruopp's classification, it is significant, if not sinister, to note how the number of problems increases as the range of interest narrows from God to society, to family and then to the self. "Always there is a black spot in our sunshine—the shadow of ourselves." [8] Truly it would seem that we human beings are like tethered animals grazing around the stake of self and shortening our range by wrapping the tether more repeatedly around the ego. This self-centeredness offers both a challenge and a temptation—a challenge to unloose "the wretch concentered all in self" and on the other hand a temptation to cater to his egoistic interests. A certain minister, rated very successful, was asked why the sermons he preached at occasions outside his parish were almost always psychological, dealing with the questions of personal happiness. He explained that in his own pulpit he varied the diet, interlarding social and expository and doctrinal sermons; but that when he went away from home to preach he took the sermons which had proven most popular. When a preacher discovers that psychological discourses are the most popular, his temptation is to specialize on them both at home and abroad. To "brighten the corner where you are" is good, but it is hardly an adequate Christian program when organized selfishness is shutting off the light from the rest of the community and hell has broken loose across the street.

In life-situation preaching we must take care to keep our messages not only true to life but as large as life. A layman

[8] Thomas Carlyle: *Sartor Resartus*, Book II, Chap. 9.

some time ago complained to a pastor after this fashion, "We men come to church seeking help for our problems and then you preachers raise so many new questions that you send us away with more problems than when we came." While we feel a certain sympathy for the man's complaint and our hearts ache for hungry sheep when they go away unfed, nevertheless the layman's criticism was not altogether valid. The minister is a teacher and the teacher's function is not merely to answer the questions which the pupils bring to school but also to lift their queries to new horizons, to arouse them to ask the right questions. Moreover the minister represents the Son of Man who "came to seek and to save that which was lost." Men are aware of some of their losses, but not of all. A man knows when he has lost his money or his health, but not always when he has lost his nerve or his social vision. A man knows when he has lost a loved one; he does not always know when he has lost his own lovableness. The task of the preacher is to demonstrate that Christlike ability which helps men to find what they have lost by losing themselves, which enables men to bear their own burdens by giving a lift to the loads of others, in the spirit of him who said paradoxically, "Come unto me, all ye that labor and are heavy-laden, and I will give you rest. Take my yoke upon you and learn of me: for I am meek and lowly of heart and ye shall find rest unto your souls." [9] To rest with a yoke, to comfort with a cross—that is the life-situation preaching needed by self-centered, comfort-loving, harmony-seekers who say they would come to church if the church would give them what they want.

In order to prevent an introspective self-centeredness and preserve the full orb of the Christian message, life-

[9] Matthew 11:28–29.

situation preaching should be blended with Biblical exposi-
tion and doctrinal teaching. If sermons aim at solving the
life situations of actual persons, they will not fall into the
traditional classifications of topical, expository, doctrinal
and the like. When we start with life situations we start
where men live, then lead the questioning soul to the doctrinal and Biblical sources. Instead of the traditional expository type of preaching which spends the first paragraphs explaining the Hebrew and Greek roots while the
listeners' minds rove over greener pastures, the sermon will
arrest the attention of the hearer with a real issue and then
direct the quest to the ever-satisfying Scriptures. It is the
project method applied to the Bible. Such preaching will
combine the teaching quality with the intensely practical.
Yet instead of reducing the "power from on high" to the
scale of our petty concerns, it leads us to the "secret place
of the Most High" where we abide "under the shadow of
the Almighty." From the vantage point of spiritual altitude
we look down on many an anxiety which had been attacking us. In the company of the Christ we are lifted out of
our littleness and emptied of our egoism.

Life situations can also be linked with the great historic
doctrines of our faith. When our personal problems are
set in the light of age-old experience, we see them in better
perspective and proportion. Our valleys are exalted and
our mountains and hills made lower when we behold them
as part of the long road which the saints have trod. Thus
instead of preaching dry sermons in defense of theological
doctrines, we bring those doctrines to our help; and our
creeds are seen not as mental strait-jackets put over on us
but as life-preservers thrown out to us.

When the message is prepared with life situations in
mind, the preacher will keep the personal element even in

the discussion of public questions. There are times when a minister feels called to deliver himself on significant current issues. But a sermon should not be so completely devoted to a social question, such as war or civic corruption or the feeding of Europe's starving children, that a hungry spirit in the congregation would find no food. The son of one of the nineteenth century's great pulpiteers reports privately that his father never preached without thinking that perhaps some one was present who was hearing the last sermon of his life. And into every message he tried to put a note which would help that individual. The son went on to remind me that in my radio congregations the number of hearers who would not be alive the following Sunday would probably be sufficient to fill a church of ordinary size. The suggestion seemed so depressing, even morbid, that I tried to relieve the gloom of the remark by saying that I realized I was preaching to a lot of "dead ones"; nevertheless, the comment of that layman has lingered in my thought to make me more sensitive to the unpredictable personal import of each sermon. In presenting special causes and public issues, the preacher should not forget that burdened, perplexed and sorrowing individuals sit before him. The sermon should never deteriorate into an impersonal topical discussion or defense of doctrine. Unless the listener leaves the church saying to himself, "That service was meant for me," for him the sermon has missed its aim.[10]

[10] My personal policy is to preach very few special sermons devoted solely to public issues, such as peace, neutrality, salacious literature, corrupt politics, share-croppers, and the like. Rather, it is my aim to take basic principles and try to swing their searchlights so that they fall upon the various phases of our social, economic, and political environment. Thus there are very few sermons which do not make a thrust at war and other current issues. Some of our most distinguished clergy devote an entire sermon to a single political or national or eco-

If life situations are kept central, the appeal of a sermon *has a wider intellectual range*. In some circles there is a spirit akin to academic snobbery which excuses the lack of popular appeal by saying that the average intellectual age is twelve years and it is impossible to put good material down to the level of morons. Sometimes a sermon is described as being over the heads of a congregation when it is really beside the point of their interest. To be sure, there are intellectual levels of preaching and the stuff passed out by some popularizers does arouse the aversion of discriminating ministers. But the trend toward class churches, both intellectual and economic, is dangerous. The loss of multitudes to the bizarre cults is appalling. It is good for people of diverse mental equipment to worship together. It makes for that accommodation which is essential to humility. With our Lord as model, we ministers should learn that true simplicity is the distilled essence of wisdom. The Roman Catholic Church endeavors to reach all classes through the universal language of symbol. But the sermon itself can deal with principles profound enough to interest the learned and in language picturesque and simple enough to hold the simple. And when the material is fused with genuine feeling, a profound sermon hides under its helpfulness the

nomic issue, thresh it through in a thorough-going fashion and thereby deliver a really significant pronouncement. Perhaps if my parish were a settled one wherein the same persons were present Sunday after Sunday and could follow through a constructive course of instruction, I too should deal with special issues in more detached and definitive fashion. But in a church at the heart of a great city, with a large proportion of transient listeners, I deem it advisable to center the sermon on some life principle or life situation and then let the radiations reflect on the current problems. In this way I try to preserve the personal element in each sermon and also bring the public problems to the attention more frequently. Furthermore I find that by repeated pricks some persons are aroused to action who take a major operation unmoved because under the anaesthetic of disagreement!

trademarks of its scholarliness. John Foster said concerning the sermons of Dr. Blair of Scotland: "They were chilled through in standing so long to be dressed." [11] Pulpit coolness may be a proof of prolonged dressing but not necessarily of spiritual or intellectual profundity. *And there is a basic difference between a parade of learning and the march of a saving message to the relief of a beleaguered soul.*

4. *Creative Compassion*

In this two-fold task of preparing the people for the word, and preparing the word for the people, the Lord's roadmaker must be motivated by creative compassion. Henry Ward Beecher once caustically commented on the unlovely attitude of certain preachers who were always on God's side against the people. All too familiar is the preacher who tries, as he says, "to put the fear of God into people," but in a way which makes both God and himself seem hostile to the people. There comes to mind an earnest young student minister who was given charge of a boys' club. He went at the job somewhat as a policeman swings into a street gang. He felt it his duty to save them, but he clearly had no affection for them. Of similar spirit are some of those who are shouting that we must "get America back to God." They say it as grimly as if they were calling in the militia to preserve order.

If we are to prepare the way of the Lord and of the people, our primary motive must not be to preserve order because we want society to be undisturbed, but rather it must be to save souls because we love people. Herein lies the fundamental difference between the reformer and the

[11] E. G. Robinson, *Yale Lectures, 1883*, p. 154.

minister of the gospel. The former is concerned to assert the moral order; the latter aims first at the redemption of the wrong-doer. At this same point is to be found the distinction between righteousness and goodness. Paul knew this difference. Fired with righteous indignation, young Saul of Tarsus had set out to rid the moral order of the subversive Christian sect. Later when his righteousness had been converted and mellowed into goodness, he wrote immortally of the love that "suffereth long and is kind." His own transforming experience throws revealing light on his statement: "For scarcely for a righteous man will one die; yet peradventure for a good man some would even dare to die." [12] Have we not all known those righteous persons whose loveless attitude arouses no desire to sacrifice for them? Not only would men not die for those grim and righteous reformers, but they would not even mourn much at their passing. On the other hand, genuine goodness kindles affection. Righteousness may generate passion, but goodness has the power of compassion. The former may destroy vices; the latter makes virtues to grow in their place.

When we convince another that we care for his welfare, we win his interest. To be interested in others is to be interesting to them. And a genuine concern cannot long be simulated. Little children are especially alert to artificial tactics. Grown children may flock for a time to hear the clever speaker who has mastered the techniques of "how to win friends and influence people," but they will not follow such a leader far in any sacrificial service; for in fact such a person lacks the essentials of leadership. A good memory, an engaging manner, an eloquent tongue, may

[12] Romans 5:7.

help to gather a congregation; but the church of the living God cannot be built by a "good mixer" unless he has the mortar of true compassion.

Compassion, to be constructive and creative, must be born of God. Natural affection prompts us to care for those within the family circle. Natural too is the give-and-take of friendship which goes on at all levels of love. The gangster who kills in cold blood has warm spots for his pals, and the most ruthless business buccaneer may be tenderly sympathetic to a favored few. Natural also is it to care for those who are lovely and lovable. Selfish and sentimental folk are fond of little children when they are nice. But what keeps teachers caring for bad boys who try their patience in a thousand ways? What can keep us caring for crowds when we see them in their subway moods, milling and pulling, ugly of temper and unruly in manner? What kept Lincoln loving and seeking to preserve this government of the people and for the people when the people were caricaturing, maligning and breaking his heart? What could keep a Christ praying for the cruel crowd which reviled him as he hung in agony on the cross?

Such compassion cannot be sustained by the sight of the people themselves. It must have a higher source of renewal. And here it is: "Love your enemies and do good, hoping for nothing again; and your reward shall be great and ye shall be the children of the Highest; for he is kind unto the unthankful and to the evil." [13] We love our fellowmen because our Heavenly Father first loved us. We love in order to be worthy children of an all-loving Father. Love for the members of God's family is caught somewhat as love is generated between brothers within the human fam-

[13] Luke 6:35.

ily. Here is a home with an only child. Then is born a new baby. This newcomer in a sense is a rival of the child already there. He competes for the affection of the parents. He divides the nursery and the playthings. He eventually will divide the patrimony. Why does not the older child resent the rivalry? At first he sometimes does. But in the natural course of events, the older child by watching the parental love and living in the atmosphere of it, begins to absorb it. And years later, if one of the brothers returns a broken prodigal to ask for reinstatement in the family circle he may even have disgraced, what is the most powerful motive for welcoming him back? Is it not, "Remember how mother loved Joe?" In the family it is the atmosphere of love which revives and sustains the often threatened brotherly love.

Likewise social brotherhood depends on the sense of Divine Fatherhood for its renewing grace. True religion is essential to effective and sustained philanthropy. Many honest social workers do not admit this. They are impatient with the methods of the church and often indifferent to its activities. And we can hardly blame them in view of the inefficiency and stupidity of the churches in some of their social and relief activities. Nevertheless, to think that vital and enduring philanthropy can be maintained without the climate of religion is as futile as to think that roses will thrive in a New York December. Henry George, the social reformer and single-taxer, was once exchanging experiences with Cardinal Manning. "I loved the people," he said, "and that love brought me to Christ as their best friend and teacher." "And I loved Christ," replied the Cardinal, "and so learned to love the people for whom he died." [14]

[14] Henry George, Jr., *Life of Henry George*, Doubleday & McClure, p. 438.

We may start with a humanitarian interest, as did Henry
George, and discover that to save men at their deepest we
need the help of the Highest. Or we may begin with the
mystical contemplation of Christ, as did the Cardinal, and
find our spirits following him out toward the circumference
of his compassion. But herein is love's true eternal triangle
—God, my brother and myself.

Not only does compassion multiply its lifting power by
running its rope through the heavenly pulley, but it thereby
also becomes joyously creative. "Joy shall be in heaven
over one sinner that repenteth, more than over ninety and
nine just persons, which need no repentance." [15] When
we perseveringly transform an unlovely sinner into a lovable character, we experience the thrill of creative work,
whereas merely keeping nice people nice is rather dull
business.

Moreover, Christlike compassion is creative because it
seeks as well as *saves* that which is lost. There is a charity,
not necessarily Christian, which begins at home. When
cases of need are laid on the door-sill, persons with the
slightest spark of humanity will respond. Primitive, pre-
Christian peoples had their code of hospitality which would
care even for an enemy once he was under the host's roof.
But the situations where sympathy is most needed are not
always thrust in our faces. The persons whose ache is the
most acute do not always cry out or come to our doors.
To go forth and seek the silent sufferers, to knock on the
doors of those so shy and reserved that they will not ask
for help, to sacrifice for the redemption of sinners unknown
to us—that is one of Christ's contributions to the world.

"The summons not to wait till they meet you on your

[15] Luke 15:7.

sheltered and orderly path, but to go forth and seek out and redeem the sinner and the fallen, the passion to heal and bring back to God the wretched and the outcast—all this I do not find in Rabbinism; that form of love seems lacking." [16] And this acknowledgment by the distinguished Jewish scholar Montefiore is paralleled by Mr. Lin Yutang who, despite his defense of the older Chinese faiths, admits that they lack a "good Samaritan spirit." Is not this lack shown in the fact that Chinese family life held together in its beautiful intricacies like rare old oriental lace but the Chinese civic and philanthropic fabric was brittle to the point of weakness? To seek as well as to save that which is lost; to hunt the hungry half way around the earth; to wince with the pain of suffering on the other side of the world—that is Christian compassion.

When the Nobile Expedition made its ill-fated attempt to reach the north pole and was wrecked, the report came back by way of Leningrad that a Swedish scientist had been left to die by two of his comrades because he could not keep up the trek. When that word reached Leningrad there was an outcry at the inhumanity of letting a man die in the snow at one's feet. But about the same time an American church was distributing food supplies to certain starvation centers in Russia. One of the Soviet Commissars came to a representative of the church and asked, "What are you Americans over here for? What are you trying to get from us? What do you want?" In these two incidents are illustrated two attitudes. In the first, the critic could understand perfectly why men should not desert a man dying at their feet—that is *humanity;* in the second, the

[16] Montefiore: "The Spirit of Judaism" in *The Beginnings of Christianity,* ed. by Jackson and Lake, Vol. I, p. 79.

critic could not understand why men should come half way round the world to rescue those dying of hunger—that is *Christianity*.

Not only has Christ's spirit lengthened the reach of compassion, but it has also quickened its ingenuity. When we love deeply enough, we develop strategy in loving. Think how a mother watches a beloved child in distress, how she waits for the moment when she can reach into that daughter's problem without doing injury to the girl's self-respect and self-reliance. Not only the desire to help but the ingenuity of helpfulness must be cultivated. It takes the gift of grace to give graciously. It requires intelligent sympathy to lift a broken human reed without bruising or weakening. It calls for infinite understanding to give back self-respect to a repentant sinner. One must have infinite patience and persevering love to follow forgiveness through so that it is not a mere condoning of the fault but a real reconciliation. He who would truly help must live with men long and closely enough to discover their deepest needs and then live near enough to God to know how to answer them. "Let us therefore come boldly unto the throne of grace, that we may obtain mercy, and find grace to help in time of need." [17] Only as we crave the mercy of God for our own sins, and catch the grace of God, as revealed in the Great Physician, are we fitted to touch with healing hand the wounds of the world.

To keep compassion creative, comprehensive and ingenious is one of the church's distinctive functions in these days when sympathies are shrinking. Our world has so many tired liberals and run-down reformers. Our world outlook has outrun our world sympathies. Foreign affairs provide the most popular luncheon topics, while foreign

[17] Hebrews 4:16.

missions are the most unpopular pulpit themes. The world's sufferings have been so repeatedly brought to our view that we have grown callous to many of them. Recall the dazed grief with which America received the news of the *Titanic* disaster with its few hundred lost. Recall the outpouring of sympathy when San Francisco and Tokio were smitten with earthquakes and fire. Remember the stunned anguish when America received the news of the bombing of Hawaii on December 7, 1941. Then contrast the response to those disasters with the calm superficial malaise caused by the reports of casualties mounting into the millions on the Russian front at about the same time. Yes, it would seem that we Americans do not wince with quite the same anguish over the blood shed by fellow humans in Europe.

Oh, to be sure, the war news makes the major headlines, but is it not mainly because we fear the war will hurt America? If the conflict had not involved us, it is doubtful how long the casualty reports would have held the front pages of our papers. In fact, it has not been uncommon to hear such expressions as this, "It would be almost a good thing if the Germans and Russians would kill one another off and thus spare the world from both evils." Life as life has been cheapened during the last three decades. The storms of world revolution have driven us a long sea mile from the compassion of the Christ.

Worse still, not only have sympathies shrunk but hatreds have sharpened. As mechanical inventiveness brings the nations closer together physically, tensions are bound to tighten unless these are dissolved in the grace of compassion. It is more popular to play on passion than to work for compassion.

We are not to be made tender by the impact of problems or by talk of vague general terms, such as humanity, brotherhood, and their like. We must first see the Heavenly Father who suffers with his children, and then we must personalize the faces behind the casualty lists and the relief rolls. The Golden Rule, to be sure, is the simple formula, but the trouble is that most persons have not the imagination to know what they would want done to them if they were in the other person's place. In this sensitizing of the imagination the church can make a major contribution through its services of worship. When men truly pray to God, "who made of one blood all nations of men for to dwell on all the face of the earth," it is like looking up into a mirror in the ceiling which enables us to see better into the places where others sit. By repeatedly exposing our minds to these outlooks and insights, we shall help to convert our secular curiosity about world affairs into a Christian compassion for their relief.

It takes a pretty high quality of goodness to feel pain for public evils, but that pain is a pretty accurate measure of a man's goodness. At one end of the moral yardstick is Pontius Pilate washing his hands, saying, "I am innocent of the blood of this just person; see ye to it." [18] At the other end is the young Jesus, so conscientious that he goes up to be baptized of John because he felt in part responsible for the sins of his people. Somewhere in the scale between the two each of us stands. Living in an immoral society, do we try to wash our hands of it, or are we willing to be baptized for it? The stain of guilt is dimmed in our own eyes by the number involved, but it is not dissolved thereby in God's sight. When a government goes to war, each individual feels that he is involved and must do something about it, that every ounce of sugar, every loaf of bread, every thrift stamp counts. But when we confront peace-time

[18] Matthew 27:24.

goals of social betterment, we have no such definiteness of individual effort and responsibility. Each admits the need and then evades it by shrugging his shoulders and saying, "But what can one person do about it?" We must sensitize the sting of social repentance and individualize the responsibility for social redemption. That is what Christ does for the conscience. He brings the world's ills home to us and leads us out in constructive compassion to "bear one another's burdens and so fulfill the law of Christ." [19]

5. *The Cure of Souls*

A basic test of the Lord's roadmaker is what our father called "the passion for souls." Such a passion grows out of a deep compassion for the persons to be reached and a profound conviction about the saving power of the gospel preached. The woeful lessening of this passion for souls in our day is due both to the cooling of compassion, for the reasons stated above, and to the losing of salvation's vivid meaning. Educated people have been thinking in the religious zones of gradual improvement and growth, the pastel shades of soul-geography; our fathers thought in terms of white and black, the clear-cut divisions of the saved and the damned. When the old-fashioned missionary of the nineteenth century held a watch in his hands and told his hearers that at every tick so many heathen went to hell, he spurred the churches with a sense of emergency and a definiteness of task. John Bunyan in his farewell sermon cried, "Dost thou see a soul that has the image of God in him? Love him, love him; say, 'This man and I must go to heaven together one day.' " [20] In those words Bunyan

[19] Galatians 6:2.
[20] *Works of John Bunyan*, John Ball & Co., Philadelphia, 1850, Vol. II, p. 283.

revealed the roots from which grew our father's recruiting zeal. But to the college-trained products who sit before today's preacher, the brimstone fires of a physical hell have been banked and the emergency calls of "Pilgrim's Progress" have been muffled.

A survey of the American religious scene reveals two groups into which the attitude toward salvation roughly divides men. On the one hand are those who might be called religious "isolationists" in the sense that they are concerned primarily with saving their own souls in a self-centered revivalistic fashion. For such it is sufficient to say, "Come to Jesus." But for the thoughtful man, their interpretation of salvation is neither worthy nor adequate. For him it is not enough to "come to Jesus"; he wants to know where he is to go with Jesus and what he is to do with Jesus. On the other hand are those whom we might term the religious "interventionists." They think of religion as a social force for the attacking of evils and the cleansing of society. But they forget that we cannot cure sickness of soul by launching a social crusade, nor can we cancel the sin of personal impurity by endowing a home for derelict women.

A layman in deep spiritual distress came recently to a minister with this question, "Have you preachers of the social gospel some views about God and prayer which you keep back from the people?" According to his story, he had been an active layman under a brilliant preacher whose voice rang with clarion confidence on social issues, but when he walked through the valley of the shadow, he turned to that pulpiteer for a personal shepherding which was not found. When sheep fall by the wayside, we cannot carry them by crying, "Wolf! wolf!" The modern minister should keep in touch with the Bureau of Social

Agencies; he should also know how to lead a soul to what our fathers called the "mourner's bench" and the "mercy seat."

The central message of Christianity is salvation. Yet the typical member of our "progressive" and "better" churches might be hard put to it to define what it means to be saved. "The glaring defect of current religion—I mean the vigorous kind, not that kind that is responsible for empty churches—is that it spends so much time in running around the arc, and rather takes the center for granted." [21] We are concerned with the accompaniments of salvation, but do not know the heart of the process. We want security both here and hereafter but that certainly is not the kernel of Christ's salvation. We crave physical health but are ignorant about the cure of souls. We desire peace of mind and peace between nations without going on into "the peace of God which passeth all understanding." We must get back to the center of our gospel. Yet we cannot return to an introverted revivalism. We must re-emphasize and reinterpret salvation for the thoughtful and the socially minded.

The expression "cure of souls" has traditionally connoted the whole priestly function of the ministerial office. But more recently the term has come to have a more specialized application. It calls to mind the relation of religion to psychology and psychiatry. A few years ago Dr. Richard Cabot of Harvard proposed that there should be two branches of theological training; first, systematic theology with all the evidence necessary to build up the student's fundamental knowledge of God and of man's relation to Him; and secondly, clinical theology, with all the technique

[21] Evelyn Underhill: *The Life of the Spirit*, Methuen & Co., London, p. 293.

essential to alleviating minds in distress. This clinical aspect of the clerical office has grown. Books on the relation between religion and psychology pour from the press. Progressive parishes maintain contact with psychiatrists.

How far can a pastor give himself to this specialized field? Almost every parish contains some cases needing mental treatment. The minister who devotes himself to this work must beware lest there be more ado in his office over the one abnormal case that responds than over the ninety and nine who need no psychoanalysis. In some parishes a minister's whole time could be monopolized by the maladjusted. There is a tendency to put too much emphasis on exploring the abnormal and not enough on developing the higher potentialities of the normal. Clinically, of course, there is a valid reason for the study of the abnormal, because therein traits are magnified to operable proportions. But this is a work for which specialized training and medical background are prerequisite. The minister, therefore, would do well to work in cooperation with competent medical advisers.

Far more profitable for the Kingdom will it be if the minister gives more emphasis to developing the normal and less to delving into the abnormal. What is it to be normal? We are inclined to measure normality by taking a Gallup poll of the traits revealed in a cross-section of the crowd. If we come up to the average, then we are normal. But a person might measure up to the highest common denominator of the crowd's composite virtues, and yet possess only a fraction of what the Great Physician calls normality. To be normal in the eyes of Christ, yes, to be saved in the Christian sense, is to have that wholeness in which we were conceived by the Creator. Dean Karl Stolz of Hartford has essayed to enumerate the marks of a normal person, as follows: He is engaged in a socially useful occupation; he is wholesomely related to other people; he is honest and capable enough to examine and improve himself: he has a sympathetic understanding of the situations of others; he cultivates a tension-reducer in the form of an avocation or hobby; he has a sound philosophy of life.[22]

Whether those six tests cover the whole circle of normality may be open to some dispute, but if we allow the Great Physician to put them to us, we shall know wherein we lack the wholeness which means salvation. Let Jesus measure the honesty of our self-examination, and we shall not parole our guilty souls in the custody of our own consciences where the guilt is soon condoned and the sin soon repeated. Let Jesus test the wholesomeness of our relations with other people to see whether we trespass on the personalities of those nearest to us and whether we meet with our friends at the level of our lower or higher interests. Let Jesus appraise our work. He does not value the "vulgar mass o'er which, from level stand," the crowd lays its market price. The Carpenter of Nazareth uncovers the underlying motivation to see whether it be the creation of values or the mere collection of rewards. Let Jesus study our philosophy of life and he will translate it from the cold realm of an intellectual formula into the force of a living comradeship.

Salvation means "coming to Jesus." Yes, but not for emotional security; rather for that wholeness which the Great Physician calls normality. In such "cure of souls" the good minister of Jesus Christ should not be dependent on the traveling evangelist or the consulting psychologist. To be sure, ministers are priestly or prophetic by temperament. Some are skilled in the art of counseling and com-

[22] Cf. Karl R. Stolz, *Tricks Our Minds Play Us*, Cokesbury, pp. 15-36.

forting, while others find their forte in public utterance. But all should seek to make their diagnoses and prescriptions in individual situations with the same definiteness of aim as does a good doctor. It should be remembered that to be a doctor of humanity is more difficult than to be a "doctor of divinity," for the former requires that a man shall culti-vate the confidences of all sorts and conditions of men, while to become the latter usually requires the cultivation of only one college president.

The Protestant doctrine of "the priesthood of all be-lievers" does not carry the assumption that believers are priests all the time. They have moments when their lips are silent, their certitude gone, and the dark night of the soul descends upon them. For this silence of the human soul the priest is needed, just as the prophet is called to give voice in the silence of God. This priestly ministry of di-vinely given sympathy makes articulate the prayers which leap through language and escape.

In our priestly office we are indebted to the psychologists for new insights, but our work is more than that of inter-preting man to himself. We are mediators between man and God. The worship of a transcendent God is more than meditation or introspection. Our Lord's prayer does not begin with introspection but with adoration: "Our Father which art in heaven, hallowed be thy name." The words give an upward stretch to the mind, an inhalation of the eternal from the far horizons. It does for our spirits what deep breathing before an open window does for the wak-ened body in the morning. As priests we help men to re-ceive the "power from on high."

In this mediation between man and God, we must be-ware that we do not make it merely an extension of ego-centricity. Recently there came to hand two books dealing with the relationship between religion and psychology.

One has quite a pious title and reads very sermonically, but its whole purport is how to *get* things from God, how to use prayer to secure what *we* want, how to become a dominant personality, how to make God the agent for achieving *our* desires. With all its religious phrases, it is simply a collection of self-centered success theories. The other book is of a different sort. It points the way to emancipation from self-centeredness. One is a book of success, the other is a book of salvation.

When we talk of bringing God to men what is our motive? A Divine Santa Claus to come down our chimneys, to fill *our* stockings which go back into *our* same old shoes and walk in *our* same old paths of self-seeking? When we pray, of whom are we thinking? Of God or of ourselves? When we open our prayers with "Our Father," do we say it as a spoiled child comes to its parent and says "father," while it is not thinking at all of the father, but only of what it wants to get from him? When we say "Hallowed be thy name," are we really thinking of God's name, or of ourselves? Those are words designed to introduce God to us, but we often make the same mistake in our introductions to God as in our introductions to other persons. It is said that one reason we do not better remember the names of persons we meet is that when we meet them, we are thinking of ourselves rather than of them. So it may be between ourselves and God. We are thinking of what we are trying to get from God and thereby fail to let Him make an impression on us. When as priests we introduce men to God, we must help men forget themselves in finding Him.

Religion as an "opiate of the people" has demonstrated its deterioration in many lands, perhaps most notably in Russia. There is now danger of repeating this tragic error in new forms of sedative. The soothing cults, sometimes misnamed healing cults, and popularizing preachers who seek to fill Sunday night pews with palatable doses of happiness pellets are reducing the surgery of the gospel into a sedative. The medical practitioners of a bygone era drugged their patients into an insensibility to pain: the modern surgeon sometimes gives a sedative to quiet the nerves of a pre-operative sufferer, and then he administers an anaesthetic at the time of the operation—but all this dulling of pain is done in prepartion for a curative removal of the root cause. The Great Physician sometimes used sedative words to calm the flustered and feverish spirits of his followers: "Come unto me, all ye that labor and are heavy laden, and I will give you rest." [23] That is the quieting stage. But listen: "Take my yoke upon you and learn of me; for I am meek and lowly in heart, and ye shall find rest unto your souls. For my yoke is easy and my burden is light." [24] Christ comforts with a yoke. He cures with a cross.

6. The Peril of the Partly Cured

In the cure of souls, as elsewhere, one of the common tragedies is the failure to follow through. So many persons have just enough contact with Christ to be half-cured. They are like the blind man of Bethsaida after Jesus' first touch. When asked, "Do you see anything?", the man replied, "I see men as trees walking." [25] Had Jesus ceased his curative work at that point, the poor fellow would have gone forth in the haze of blurred vision. He would have been able to discern the outlines of men but not their features. He would have gone around with his objective en-

[23] Matthew 11:28.
[24] *Ibid.*, 11:29-30.
[25] Mark 8:24.

vironment all out of focus. His would have been the tragedy of the half-cured.

Think of those who have felt a first touch of Christ, sufficient to open their eyes to his way of life, but have not followed through until their vision is properly focused.

It is interesting to follow the footsteps of Jesus and see how frequently the gospels record that the people were amazed or astounded. They wondered at the authority of his words. They marveled at the manifestations of his power. But that is as far as the impression seemed to go. The Master said to them rebukingly: "Having eyes, see ye not? And having ears, hear ye not?" Some of them, of course, were blinded by prejudice. They refused to see. But many, I have no doubt, looked, and were too indifferent to inquire further into the secret of his power. They were like a certain acquaintance of mine who greets almost every statement made to her with the expression: "Well, what do you know about that?" Now, that exclamation sounds like a question. But it is not. She does not really want to know what you know about that. If you started to tell her what you know, she would not listen. She just opens her eyes in the presence of a new idea, but she does not focus her gaze on it sufficiently to see it clearly.

In every classroom teachers will tell you how few among the students really listen. They may all be sitting with their eyes open. Some have a look of bland indifference. Others have a kind of big baby stare of wonderment. Then there are the few who have a searching intensity to their gaze. They are the select few who belong to what Halford Luccock calls "the aristocracy of the attentive." They are the ones who will follow through to explore the subject further. From this group come the inventors, the discoverers, the real scholars.

So is it with a congregation as the gospel is being preached. All those present may have their eyes open—more or less—but only a few have that intentness of gaze which indicates that their attention is really focused and they will follow the subject further. In one prominent university of America there is a custom that those who wish to ask the preacher any further questions may go with him to a room and talk it over. This academic version of the old evangelistic "after-meeting" may not result in many "conversions" but it does help to clear and confirm some convictions.

So often men stop with just a vague hazy view of even Christ himself. Practically every one has a general impression of Jesus. They know the beautiful story of Bethlehem and the Golden Rule which he taught us. They are familiar with the parables of the Prodigal Son and the Good Samaritan. They know that Palm Sunday commemorates Christ's royal entry into Jerusalem; Good Friday, his crucifixion; and Easter Sunday, his triumph over death. But so comparatively few focus their thought on Christ long enough to comprehend the sweep of his lordship, to peer into the meaning of his atoning death, or to see the bridge between his life and ours.

Or consider how hazy is the common view of the Bible. They have a few favorite passages. They have some general vague ideas about the "Good Book," as they call it. But have they focused their study on it long enough to get the meaning back of the story of Eden, or to see the sweep of the divine drama of Israel's history from the patriarchs through the law and the prophets, through the exodus and the exile down to the coming of One whom six hundred million now call the Christ? Do they understand the unfolding of revelation which explains why in one period it was right to say, "an eye for an eye and a tooth for a tooth," while in a later period the divine order was, "Love your enemies"?

So, too, our views of our fellow men are blurred. We see our brothers not as individuals, but as a vague mass called humanity. We, like the blind man in the Gospel record, see men not personally but in the mass as trees moving.

The tragedy of these vague views is not merely that we miss the satisfaction of knowing more; but these half-visions and half-truths are so dangerous. When our view of the Bible is so vague, any little flippant skeptic can toss us out of the ark of faith into the sea of doubt. When our view of Christ is so hazy, we can be misled into following almost any erratic interpretation of him. When our view of the church is so partial and parochial any little parish squabble can shake our belief in the Body of Christ. When our view of men is so unclear, we can be so cruel. The person with his eyes open but not focused is a spiritual peril to himself and others. He needs to see life steadily and to see it whole. He needs the second touch of the Great Physician.

A second group of the half-cured is composed of those who have had enough contact with the Christ to catch his aspirations but not enough to feel his inspiration. The first glimpse of the Great Physician stirs our aspirations. His winsome goodness awakens in us a hunger and thirst after righteousness. His lofty ideals make us restless in our low compromises. His superb mastery of pain and hardship make us eager to know the secret of his strength.

The report is that Rubinstein when visiting once in New York City was asked by his host if he would like to attend church. He replied, "Yes, if you will take me to hear a preacher who will tempt me to do the impossible." That is what a truly Christian minister should do—set us seeking a perfection ever beyond us, start us toward flying goals which ever elude our grasp, lead us to the rock that is higher than we, from which we glimpse a height that is higher. Christ has filled the hearts of men with aspiration after personal goodness, racial brotherhood, industrial justice, world peace.

But pause a moment. To be ever aspiring may prove exhausting business, unless it be supplemented by inspiration. Aspiration shows us the goal and the distance to it; inspiration encourages with a view of how far we have come. Aspiration gives us the map of the journey; inspiration furnishes the music to keep us marching.

Christ came to give us both, and both are so desperately needed today. Our aspirations must be kept on edge. We dare not lose sight of the lofty goals of peace and justice, liberty and brotherhood. If we let down our ideals in these days of darkness, we are lost. Yet when I think of some of the young people in my parish, I feel that they need inspiration even more than aspiration. They have ambition, they have high ideals; but they feel they are not getting anywhere. What they need is encouragement, something to inspire them with hope. And when I turn toward the middle-aged folk, I see so many who have loosened their moral harness and allowed their spirits to lag. They need an awakening of the will and conscience to new ideals, but even more they need the inspiration of feeling that their work and efforts are worth-while.

Christ came not only to arouse a smug publican like Levi out of his comfortable compromising job and transform him into a comrade of the unending quest. He came also to lift up the broken-hearted Magdalene and restore her faith in herself. "A bruised reed shall he not break, and smoking flax shall he not quench, till he send forth judgment unto victory." [26]

Let us turn now to a third group of the half-cured—those who have enough contact with Christ to be decent, but not enough to be dynamic. The first impact of Christ's life upon a person is to arouse a sense of decency. In the clear light of his character our deeds look as shoddy as stage jewelry, which pass for gems under the limelight but reveal their cheapness in the sunlight. He awakens in us the desire for the things that are true, honorable, just and of good report. But some persons seem to spend all their strength in the effort to be decent. They manage to keep themselves fairly upright. They walk the taut line of the Ten Commandments without falling off. But in doing so they resemble the tight-rope walker who succeeds in keeping his footing on the swaying rope. He gets across from one end to the other, but he does not appear to have much energy left for carrying any weight with him. So it is with some persons. It is such a strain for them to keep decent that they have no energy for helping others.

Such a person is only a half-cured Christian. The healthy follower of Christ has an athletic spirit which carries his virtues with such easy grace that he makes goodness attractive to others and has a surplus of strength for serving others. Jesus tried so hard to help his disciples through the stage of tension where it took all their strength just to be good. He wanted them to be not only good but radiantly joyous in their goodness. He saw that this required an inner singleness of purpose.

The guide to God must possess the skill of the second touch. He must have the patience to see men through the

[26] Matthew 12:20.

fog of their cloudy thinking. He must be able to pray men through their incoherent doubts and their intolerant dogmatisms. He must be a leader who not only awakens aspiration to start men going but imparts inspiration to keep them going. He must be an interpreter who can reopen the chapters of past personal history and recover the picture of the man one intended to be and also cut the pages of the future with his imagination and show the man one still can be. He must be a physician who puts his finger on the weak spot without rubbing it in. He must have sympathy for men's wounded feelings and yet not succumb to the softness of which Swinburne spoke when he said of one preacher, "For tender minds he served up half a Christ." The good minister of the gospel must seek to give the whole Christ to the half-cured who need to be made whole.

7. Custodians of the Crises

As long as ministers are custodians of the crises of life, they have unparalleled opportunity for the cure of souls. Men seek the church at those moments when life is most real; when they come to link life with life at the marriage altar, their eyes misty with love and mysterious with purpose: when they bring the fruit of their bodies to the baptismal font for dedication, sensing the sacredness of life and sobered by the responsibility of it; when they come for consolation in the shattering hour of death. We are the privileged disciples who ascend with men at such moments into their Mount of Transfiguration. Can we interpret to their wondering eyes the glimpses of the eternal? [27]

To take the high mood of the marriage altar and trans-

[27] Cf. Author's *Live for Tomorrow*, Chap. 6.

mute it into lasting loyalty for the making of a home; to stand with men in the dark hours when "deep calleth unto deep" and to do for them what Richard Cobden did for John Bright when he translated the latter's personal sorrow into public service; to visit men when the breaks in health have taken them out of the stream of activity and to show them where the real current flows as distinguished from the eddies in which they have been immersed; to impart the secret of victorious vision which sees through the breaks in life to the things that abide—these are among our high functions as custodians of the crises of life. The question for us is, can we show ourselves faithful stewards of the mysteries of God, keeping the mystery without losing the wonder? The repetition of sacred moments and sacramental functions must not be allowed to beget a perfunctory professionalism which imparts to the minister the facile and unfeeling manner of an undertaker. When the Lord's representative no longer feels the thrill of his parishioner's high moments and the anguish of their sorrows, he not only loses his shepherding appeal but it is evidence that he has lost his spiritual touch.

8. *Preparing the Way of the People*

And if we are to prepare the way of the people as well as the way of the Lord, we must give a closing glance at the task of social roadmaking. In the medical profession there is the field of preventive medicine and public health. Likewise the cure of souls has its public and preventive side. To train youth in the personal virtues without purifying the social conditions in which they must apply those principles; to prepare youth in confirmation classes without concerning oneself about the industrial system which may brutalize them or the war system which may butcher them —is a short-sightedness which is nothing less than sin.

Listen to the prophet's command: "Prepare ye the way of the people; cast up, cast up the highway; gather out the stones, lift up a standard for the people." [28] That is our task. The preparing of the way of the people to our God is similar to the building of a highway through the wilderness. First, the engineers who mark the lines; then the blasters who remove the rocks; then the construction force which lays the road. By temperament and training we ministers qualify for one of these three tasks. Some of us are seers, prophetic spirits, social engineers who see far ahead of the crowd and chart the course of advance. Others of us are good at blasting. We revel in attacking entrenched prejudices, in removing stubborn obstructionists, in laying axes at the roots of fruitless institutions. Others of us have the pastoral temperament, fitted to make the paths for little children, to lay the roads for the burdened travelers, to build the broad highway for the crowd. "But all these worketh that one and the self-same spirit. But now are they many members, but one body. And the eye cannot say unto the hand, 'I have no need of thee'; nor again the head to the feet, 'I have no need of you.'" [29]

We are all one body in Christ. And let us thank God that the church, the body of Christ, is now developing these diversities of gifts. Let us who are pastors uphold the hands of the social prophets and experts who are charting the course of Christ far beyond the paved roads of conventional morality. And let the social prophets and seers be

[28] Isaiah 62:10.
[29] I Corinthians 12:11, 20, 21.

patient with the pastors who are faithfully trying to bring their flocks up to the advance positions. If we can work together, tomorrow will find the crowd traveling where the prophet walks today.

Chapter V

THE LEAST IN THE KINGDOM

For I say unto you, Among those that are born of women there is not a greater prophet than John the Baptist; but he that is least in the Kingdom of God is greater than he.

Luke 7:28

He can bring thy Summer out of Winter, though thou have no Spring. Now God comes to thee, not as in the dawning of the day, not as in the bud of the Spring, but as the Sun at noon to illustrate all shadows, as the sheaves in harvest, to fill all penuries, all occasions invite his mercies, and all times are his seasons.

John Donne, Sermon II from
Eighty Sermons, 1640

THE LEAST IN THE KINGDOM

1. *The Kingdom of Heaven Is at Hand—But Where?*

The religious and social tensions of Palestine at the time of Jesus reveal some parallels to those in America of our day. The shadow of Caesar fell athwart the Mediterranean world. The advance of the Roman legions engulfed nation after nation in the Near East. The hope of restoring the Davidic line in Israel grew dimmer and dimmer. Only the most fanatical still cherished that dream; but that there still were some of this mind was shown by the nationalistic Messianism which broke out sporadically following the Maccabean dynasty. Opposed to the fanatical nationalists were the Sadducees, the political appeasers who sought a comfortable compromise with the Roman overlords.

While there were these two alternatives in political action, there was a religious attitude which formed a third course. That was the position taken by those who hoped for direct divine intervention. These were the Apocalyptists. Taking the traditional teachings of the post-exilic prophets at face value, they would wait upon the Lord, trusting him to bring his will to pass. They would prepare for God's intervention by repentance and good works: but they need not raise a hand to hasten the event. This event was to be more than a restoration of the Davidic kingship; it was cosmic in its proportions with Israel at the center of the world outlook. In addition to those who would wait passively for the Parousia, there were the ascetics who sought a way out of the political impasse by retreating into the desert or by imposing on themselves rigorous restrictions and rites.

And then into the midst of this apocalypticism and asceticism, came another strain, the revival of ancient prophecy. Israel's prophets had ever been produced by times of tension. The time was ripe for another. The people that sat in darkness were looking for a great light and listening for a voice that would awaken the memories of the great days of Elijah and Isaiah. Into the atmosphere, electric with expectation of another prophecy, flashed the figure of John the Baptist.

While Matthew reports John as introducing his message with the words: "Repent ye for the Kingdom of Heaven is at hand," [1] the omission of this utterance in the other gospels leads to the belief that it may be editorial. At least John shows no concern elsewhere for the kingdom concept. Malachi 4:5 links the revival of prophecy with the coming of the Day of the Lord: "Behold, I will send you Elijah the prophet before the coming of the great and dreadful day of the Lord." The Day of the Lord carried no such connotation to the Hebrew mind as that contained in Jesus' picture of the kingdom. John's message might be summed up thus: *"Repent, for the day of judgment is coming."*

John's method and message of preparation *for the Day of the Lord* differed at many points from the Jesus way of working. John was remote and ascetic; Jesus mingled with men and made friends. John talked down to the people; Jesus took little children up in his arms. John made people want to hide for their safety; Jesus wooed people out of

[1] Matthew 3:1.

their cellared existence into the sunshine of hope. John was tense, hurrying toward his goal; Jesus never gave the impression of being hurried, taking time to talk with dejected women at wells and to join with families at wedding feasts. John was primarily a critic; Jesus was a creator. John's idea of the Messianic method was to lay the "axe at the root of the tree" and cut out; Jesus likened himself to a gardener standing before a barren fig tree and pleading for more time to dig around the tree that he might make it bear fruit. John saw the evil lurking behind the hypocrisies of men and cried, "O generation of vipers, who hath warned you to flee from the wrath to come?" [2] Jesus saw the goodness hidden behind the sullen face of a publican Zaccheus and the soiled soul of a Magdalene and sought to call it forth.

Withal, however, John was great enough to recognize his limitations. "I indeed baptize you with water unto repentance; but he that cometh after me is mightier than I, whose shoes I am not worthy to bear: He shall baptize you with the Holy Ghost and with fire." [3] John's baptism was thus only a promise and a hope. He looked forward to that which he could not impart. He perceived that Jesus was the agent of a righteousness superior to his own and that this higher goodness was somehow linked with a gift of the Holy Spirit. John saw himself as a roadmaker leading men to the threshold of something he could not give, and the greatness of his spirit was revealed in his remark: "He must increase, but I must decrease." [4]

Across that threshold lay the Kingdom of God or the Kingdom of Heaven which was the focal feature of Jesus'

[2] Matthew 3:7.
[3] *Ibid.*, 3:11.
[4] John 3:30.

message. The Kingdom of Heaven is a term which has lost its tang for the modern churchman. It is a generalization which has become so broad that it is flat. But suppose that we had never heard of Christ or of the Christian religion and were to pick up the New Testament for the first time. What would be most likely to excite our curiosity? We would see a young carpenter turned prophet going about Galilee "preaching the gospel of the Kingdom." He was on fire with his theme. He was always talking about it, always trying to explain it. In one image after another, he was insisting that it is the greatest thing in life; that it is the pearl of great price for which the discoverer will gladly sacrifice everything he possesses; in short, that its possession means the life that is life indeed.

We would be mystified by the secret of this kingdom as we watched how Jesus himself seemed unable to find words adequate to describe it. His matchless parables were unforgettable and yet they were untranslated by their hearers into the reality which Jesus was trying to impart. They did not comprehend how his kingdom could be in the world and yet not of the world. But as we watched Jesus, we would see, as did his hearers, that he was talking about something utterly real to himself. He spoke as one having authority. He was describing what he had experienced. We would see that he "had something." And would we not grow excitedly eager to know what is the Kingdom of Heaven?

The followers of Jesus at first thought that he meant to establish an earthly Kingdom. In my opinion the most plausible explanation of the betrayal was Judas' belief that thereby he would force the hand of Jesus and compel the Master to manifest the divine power which was at his command. That Jesus' interpretation of the Kingdom impressed his contemporaries as this-worldly rather than other-worldly is indicated from the fact and manner of his execution. He was not stoned to death but crucified, a Roman not a Jewish penalty. The Jewish authorities may have instigated his death, but the fact remains that he suffered the penalty reserved for revolutionists and other male-factors against the Roman regime. The kingdom which he proclaimed was interpreted in a political sense by the Roman authorities.

Pilate, of course, did not comprehend Jesus' conception of the Kingdom. Our Lord knew it was futile to attempt an explanation in Pilate's court. And the sign "King of the Jews" which was nailed on the cross was a cruel mockery. Jesus claimed no earthly kingship. In fact, the Kingdom of God, as he conceived it, had no room for a messianic king. It was a pure theocracy, the direct control of the universe and its events by God Himself. "It is God's Kingdom, God's reign, not the kingdom or reign of some anointed representative of God, which is Jesus' great and continual concern: and certainly it is no dream of his own personal dominion over the nations that interests him and forms the subject of his teaching." [5]

The delayed coming of such a kingdom drove believers away from it in two directions. On the one hand, it aroused the doubts of John the Baptist by seeming too anarchic.

---

[5] Frederick C. Grant, *The Gospel of the Kingdom*, Macmillan, p. 128. Does this fact not serve to throw light on two utterances of Jesus which have often been contrasted? Of the rival healer, he said: "Forbid him not, for he that is not against us is for us" (Luke 9:50). To the neutral onlookers he said: "He that is not with me is against me" (Luke 11:23). In the first, Jesus was concerned only with the service to the Kingdom of God and not with the recognition of himself. In the second he was condemning those who would not join with him in serving the Kingdom of God: and so all-inclusive is God's Kingship that there can be no neutrality.

He had expected a near-at-hand day of judgment with the Christ sifting the wheat from the chaff, and he sent to inquire of Jesus: "Art thou he that should come? Or look we for another?" [5a] On the other hand, the trend of interpretation among Jesus' followers was toward the purely apocalyptic and transcendental. "My Kingdom is not of this world." [6] "Flesh and blood cannot inherit the Kingdom of God." [7] Then as the apocalyptic dream faded through long delays, the church came virtually to take the place of the kingdom. We know the sad story of the imperial church, whose interest in self-aggrandizement led to the neglect of general social welfare. When Protestantism came on the scene, it was passionate to correct ecclesiastical abuses, but it had no universal transforming mission. In its social program it became the arm of the secular government. The Kingdom of God was shifted from earth to heaven, as a refuge from a world which both church and state could not hope to fashion in the divine pattern.

Nevertheless the Kingdom could not be kept on a purely transcendent plane. The prayer, "Thy Kingdom come," is embedded in the heart of man as in the heart of our Lord. Here and there sporadic groups sought to bring the kingdom pattern down to earth. Monastic communities gathered to themselves seekers after a devout and harmonious group life. When Cassian asked the anchorites of Europe why they had come to the desert, they replied, "We have come to seek the Kingdom of God." Protestantism also produced sects, such as the Waldensians, Mennonites and Quakers, who essayed to build their communities after the "pattern showed when in the mount." America has seen

[5a] Luke 7:19.
[6] John 18:36.
[7] I Corinthians 15:50.

the sprouting of several ideal commonwealths. Thus for over eighteen hundred years the segregated method of establishing the Kingdom was tried without permanent success.

Then in the latter part of the last century came the conception of the Kingdom of Heaven as a universal social pattern, not interposed by divine intervention but evolved by human cooperation. The advancing industrial development, the extravagant optimism of the physical sciences, the expanding culture and "humanities" all served to reinforce the confidence in the evolutionary theory. The English voices of Maurice, Kingsley, Ruskin and others mingled with the American prophecies of Josiah Strong, Walter Rauschenbusch, Charles R. Brown, Washington Gladden and others to proclaim the possibility of realizing a Christlike social order. That hope fired the imaginations of students. It gave impetus to a new religious journalism. It spread settlement houses over our cities in mushroom growth. It opened the entrances of the dark continents to Christendom's medicine, agriculture, and gospel whereby the will of God might be done "on earth as it is in heaven."

But now there are those who regard those expectations as the rubbish of a discarded liberalism. Theological precincts are being fumigated to rid them of any remaining traces of liberalism in order that we may breathe the air of realism, which attests its purity by the acrid odor of a sulphurous pessimism. In a recent symposium of European and American interpreters we have such conclusions as these: From C. H. Dodd: "The future . . . is not our concern, nor is it in the future that we must seek the perfection of which the temporal order is not capable, but in the other world in which the ultimate meaning of history resides." From Paul Tillich we learn that progress in morality is deemed impossible, and even "approximation to the final fulfilment would replace fulfilment by the way to it, and thus is ultimately self-contradictory." Edwyn Bevan repudiates the idea of "the non-Christian optimistic humanitarian hope" as incompatible with the Christian attitude toward the world and warns against "supposing that it is possible for us to trace any progressive approximation in the course of history to the Kingdom of God." [8] This school of interpreters would have us believe that "right is forever on the scaffold" and "wrong forever on the throne" until the God, who stands within the shadow, transfers by a supreme act of power the issues to a super-historical realm where the demonic forces do not exist.

2. *The Kingdom That Is Here*

But amid all these fluctuations of interpretation we cannot forget that Jesus talked about the Kingdom of Heaven as a reality already here. "Blessed are the poor in spirit for theirs is"—not is to be—"the Kingdom of Heaven." [9] To a certain scribe who answered correctly concerning the commandments of love to God and love to neighbor, Jesus said, "Thou art not far from the Kingdom of God." Clearly he was referring to no super-historical or post-resurrection state. "The Kingdom of God cometh not with observation. Neither shall they say, Lo here! or lo, there! for behold, the Kingdom of God is within you." [10] Here was a reality not perceived by the senses, yet more real than the sensuous.

As in the case of other deep realities which cannot be captured in definitions, the meaning of the Kingdom is best

[8] *The Christian Century*, August 10, 1938. Review of *The Kingdom of God and History* by H. G. Wood *et al.*, Willett Clark and Co.
[9] Matthew 5:3.
[10] Luke 17:20-21.

approached by watching those who possess it. "Blessed are the poor in spirit, for theirs is the Kingdom of Heaven." Who are the "poor in spirit"? They are those who do not insist on their rights, who do not make demands on what they meet. They do not ask what use they can derive from a thing, but they try to appreciate it for what it is in itself. The poor in spirit are those who paradoxically get the goodness of a thing because they do not think what good they are going to get out of it.

This paradoxical principle may be observed, for instance, in relation to music. If a person go to hear an opera in order to be able to discuss it at a forthcoming dinner party, or to broaden his general culture, or to be seen by his fellow box-holders, or to relax his nerves in the interest of his health—if he is trying to get the good of the opera for any such self-interested ends, he will not enter fully into the beauty of the music. If one is to enter into the enjoyment of the composer's work, he must forget himself and his demands, and allow himself to fall in love with the music. Beauty is a kingdom to which one must become selflessly subject. Only as he surrenders to its spell can he enter into its enjoyment.

This requirement for admission holds good when we turn from the realm of art to the sphere of science. The progress of science has been hindered at every step by those practical persons who asked of each new experiment, "What is the use of it?" The hard-headed business men, even the academicians, sneered at Galileo as they saw him dropping objects from Pisa's leaning tower in his effort to test the relationship between weight and speed. No doubt they said, "What good will it do him when he discovers it?" Yet as it has turned out, the inventions and discoveries of greatest use originated in experiments motivated by no practical purpose. No truths have been more useful in the long human struggle than those utterly abstract truths which we call mathematical. Yet they were discovered and evolved by men who saw no use in them and they would not have been found at all if the aim had been to make use of them. When we say that "necessity is the mother of invention," we must interpret necessity in no narrow practical sense but make it include that deep need of the human soul to know the truth for the sake of truth. Truth is a kingdom which belongs to those who give themselves to it, lead where it may, cost what it will, use or no use.

And this law of entrance is the same in love, as in art or science. Possessive love, whether legalized by marriage or not, is only a pale imitation of love's reality. Lust, which often masquerades for love, is merely self-love trying to satisfy itself in simulated affection for its object. In real love, the lover is swept off his feet; he is lifted out of himself. It is something he surrenders to, something he forgets himself in. Love is a kingdom which belongs to the poor in spirit, who are not asking for their own rights or looking for their own profit, but who give themselves gratefully in self-surrender.

Even the most earth-bound creatures have had some glimpses into one or more of these kingdoms. Some have been lifted out of themselves by listening to some great symphony or by looking at some masterpiece of painting. Some have experienced the thrill of the scholar in the pursuit of truth when physical hunger was forgotten and the joy of the search banished all thought of its profit. Some have known the ecstasy of falling in love. These realms are present realities. Yet the experiencing of them eludes our limited language. Those who know them can testify of the

fact in analogies and parables. But only the initiates understand the passwords. "Every one that is of the truth heareth
my voice." [11]

And now is not the Kingdom of Heaven the unity or
universe of these ultimate goods, beauty, truth, love, goodness? Was not Jesus trying to tell his hearers that these
realms into which we get occasional fleeting glimpses can
become our natural zones of living, if we become sufficiently poor in spirit to surrender ourselves to their spell?
Can we not test for ourselves the expansive enrichment of
life which comes when we cease looking for the use and
profit of things and give ourselves to the enjoyment of
friends, the deep satisfactions of family blessings, the companionship of little children, the dewy freshness of new
days, the ageless creations of art, the glory of autumnal
forests, the contemplation of the goodness of the God who
made them all? These are realities within our reach, here
and now. They go to form the Kingdom of God which is
within us and around us. Unfortunately the word "Kingdom" suggests a region or realm with boundaries. The term
"Kingship of God" is better, for the only bounds to the
appropriation of these divine gifts are those which man
sets by his own attitudes.

The Kingdom of God is within us as health is in the
body. "For God hath not given us the spirit of fear; but of
power and of love and of a sound mind." [12] Doctors admit
that their work is primarily to clear away the barriers to the
healing powers resident within the body. Similarly the
Great Physician sought to release the imprisoned splendor
which he saw lurking behind the soiled curtains of the Magdalene's sordid life. To him the renegade publican Zaccheus

[11] John 18:37.
[12] II Timothy 1:7.

was still a "son of Abraham" with the roots of righteousness still in him awaiting the gardener's spade. To Jesus the prodigal in the far country "came to himself" when he rose from the husks with a hunger for his father's house. In each, the Kingdom of God is an inner health or goodness to be released. It is "the power that worketh in us" waiting to come to its own. And to bring in the Kingship of God is to clear away the barriers which our diseased desires have erected.

We are ringed around with egocentric ramparts which shut out the rule of God. Just as when a candle is brought near to an ancient silver mirror, the multitudinous fine lines, wrought by much polishing, arrange themselves in concentric circles around the point of light, so egocentric man centers the large interests of life around his own point of use or profit, causing humanity to appear, as Hobbes said, "solitary, poor, nasty, brutish and short." Self-centeredness is a *cul de sac* which shuts man off from the exhilaration of great enterprises, the delights of disinterested helpfulness, the enlargements of cooperating comradeship, the delivering resources of the Divine Presence. To get ourselves out of the way is the requisite for realizing the Kingship of God.

To say that we let out the Kingdom which is within us is not to minimize the sinfulness of the natural man or the necessity of divine intervention for man's redemption. The Kingdom is "prepared from the foundation of the world" [13] but so also is the gravity of sinful desire. In the midst of life we are in death. The processes of decay hound the energies of growth. The divine image embedded in us by the Creator is marred by the meshwork of inherited and accumulated sinfulness. "O wretched man that I am! Who shall

[13] Matthew 25:34.

deliver me from the body of this death?" [14] That is the cry of the same man whom we have quoted as saying, "God hath not given us the spirit of fear, but of power and of love and of a sound mind." [15] But Paul, who knew the awful tension of inner goodness dammed against the barriers of perverse desire, went on to say, "I thank God through Jesus Christ our Lord." [16] The Son of Man is come to seek and to save the Kingdom of God which is lost within us.

Jesus recognized the existence of both eternal and indestructible forces of which man's life is composed, that is both the force of his animal nature and the force of his consciousness of divine kinship. Saying little of the animal force which is independent of human will, Jesus stressed the sense of divine kinship, calling upon man to know it more closely, to set it free from its retarding barriers and to carry it to a higher degree of intensity. In the process of liberating and intensifying this force, the true life of man consists.

"The divine perfection is the asymptote of human life to which it is always striving and always approaching although it can only be reached in infinity. Men cannot know when the day and the hour of the Kingdom of God will come because its coming depends on themselves alone. The answer is like that of the wise man who, when asked whether it was far to the town, answered, 'Walk.' How can we tell whether it is far to the goal which humanity is approaching when we do not know how men are going towards it, when it depends on them whether they go or

[14] Romans 7:24.
[15] II Timothy 1:7.
[16] Romans 7:25.

do not go, stand still, slacken their pace, or hasten it? All we can know is what we who make up mankind ought to do and not to do to bring about the coming of the Kingdom of God. And that we all know. And we need only each begin to do what we ought to do; we need only each live with all the light that is in us to bring about at once the promised Kingdom of God to which every man's heart is yearning." [17]

3. *The Kingdom That Is Coming Here*

The Kingdom of Heaven, which is within us as is the healing blood that pulses against the walls of our arteries, is also around us as the waves which beat against the shore. The influences of the transcendent God impinge upon us at every pore of the human spirit. "In him we live and move and have our being." [18] The Kingdom of God can come and the will of God can be done "on earth as it is in heaven." It comes not as something foreign to this earth interposed by divine intervention, nor as something to be built by man's efforts, but as a potential presence to be realized by removing the barriers and letting it spread. When we see how one godly spirit can leaven a whole household or how a half dozen spiritual leaders can lift the tone of a whole town, who will set limits to the social spread of the Kingdom?

Making allowance for relapses and admitting retrogression on several sectors during the last few decades, my reading of history reveals traces of progress which I interpret as marks of God's growing kingship. From the muddy cave of the savage to the Taj Mahal and the Chartres Ca-

[17] Leo Tolstoy: *The Kingdom of God*, William Heinemann, London, Vol. II, pp. 136–137.
[18] Acts 17:28.

thedral; from the grunts of African tribes to the sessions of scientists on a university campus; from the groaning of slaves in Egypt to the broadcasting of Parsifal into the humblest home in America—these are evidences of refinement which suggest progress and purpose. To be sure, scientists can still be turned into savage war-makers, motors can be transformed into tanks, air transports can become bombers dropping death on babies—but the standards by which we judge these things are rising and the values of life are being lifted. In all this I see a God working to redeem the world and not a God merely waiting to receive the refugees from an unredeemed society.

Let us then admit that we have been prodigal sons of an indulgent liberalism, dwelling in a far country of fantastic humanitarian hopes. We know now that the hungers of men cannot be satisfied with the husks of humanism. But when we turn to seek God's kingdom let us also remember that he does not wait for us in some realm beyond history, but that he seeth our returning afar off and cometh forth to meet us. Or to modernize the figure, let us abandon the idea of inevitable progress as an escalator lifting us to the Kingdom; but in stepping off the escalator we do not need to take the coal chute to the cellar. We can still take the stairs of hope, climbing not as those who trust their own strength, but as those who would "work out [their] own salvation with fear and trembling" knowing that "it is God which worketh in [us] both to will and to do of his good pleasure." [19]

For theologians and moralists to repudiate the Kingdom of God as this-worldly would *depress* the nerves of social effort, but it would not *destroy* them. Man's ineradicable desire to realize a Christlike order would break out again

[19] Philippians 2:12, 13.

in sporadic and segregated communities. Perhaps that is what we are to see in our day—a revival of monastic groups, of Brook Farm experiments, of ashrama, and other cells in which men seek the ideal community. After the Napoleonic wars came a revival of monasticism in the church of England.[20] And if defeatism kills all hope of making the world safe for democracy or keeping democracy safe in the world, men will retreat from the world in the hope of building beloved communities for those willing and able to share it. If it is not possible to realize the Kingdom of God in history, it is equally impossible to confine it to the hereafter. The Kingdom of Heaven is within us, and it strives to find social expression as irrepressibly as does love or any of the other longings within our natures.

The Kingdom of God in its *perfection* is beyond history: in its *approximation* it is within history. It is both present and future. It is at hand now in this world of cruelty even as love is at hand even when it is being crucified. The Kingdom comes gradually as a mustard seed grows: yet it comes suddenly as a flood or a thief in the night. The Kingdom is God's gift; yet we must work for it, as one seeks for a pearl of great price. The pearls of the Kingdom are not cast before swine but are given only to those able to receive. The Kingdom comes at the behest of a transcendent God: but when the Son of Man shall come in his glory and say, "Come, ye blessed of my Father, inherit the Kingdom prepared for you from the foundation of the world," [21] that inheritance is bestowed, not on the supine sitters, but on the righteous who have been preparing for it by their service to the hungry, the imprisoned, even the least.

[20] Cf. Author's *Revival of the Conventual Life in the Church of England in the Nineteenth Century*, Doctor's Thesis, Columbia University, 1917.
[21] Matthew 25:34.

Let us stop talking, therefore, about *building the Kingdom* and start preaching as never before about *realizing the Kingdom*. Admitting that the complete and perfect rule of God as conceived by Jesus is an absolute never to be fully realized in history, nevertheless that ideal should serve to inspire social effort, not to paralyze it. It is a mountain peak that lures us and not a mirage that deceives us. Its ever elusive perfection will prevent man from ascribing divine sanction to social programs and panaceas which reflect the brightness of men but not the wisdom of God. It will humble the pride of the social reformer who sees in his particular scheme the chief plank in the Kingdom platform. It will serve as a source of divine discontent with any social program, but it will sustain the social idealists with the faith that the seekers of the Kingdom who have gone before were not deluded, but that "they having obtained a good report through faith receive not the promise; God having provided some better thing for us, that they without us should not be made perfect." [22] Wherefore, believing that we are "workers together with God" for a Kingdom which can come on earth as in heaven, we can the better "run with patience the race that is set before us, looking unto Jesus the author and finisher of our faith." [23]

In the light of this we need not be troubled to explain away Jesus' recorded remark concerning John the Baptist: "He that is least in the Kingdom of God is greater than he." [24] This was no slighting rebuke of his great forerunner, whom he had just praised. It was no reflection on John's moral achievement, nor did it put the Baptist outside the pale of the redeemed in the hereafter, as some seem to fear.

[22] Hebrews 11:39, 40.
[23] *Ibid.*, 12:1, 2.
[24] Luke 7:28.

It was our Lord's kindly and patient announcement that
John, with all his mighty work, did not comprehend the
immanence of the Kingdom nor the method of realizing it.
John worked for the coming of the Kingdom, but he did
not know how to receive it. He felt the Lord was at hand,
but he did not comprehend Christ's way of practising the
presence of God.

John, the forerunner, bears no blame for this lack of
understanding; but we who have had nineteen centuries to
study "the way, the truth, and the life," have no alibi for
our failure to comprehend. Yet, as Evelyn Underhill says,
we mostly spend our lives conjugating three verbs: "to
want, to have, and to do"; forgetting that these have no
significance except as they are included in the verb, "to be."
Our activism and possessivism keep us from appropriating
the Living Reality which stands at the door and knocks.[25]
"From the days of John the Baptist until now the Kingdom
of Heaven suffereth violence," [26] despite the teaching of
Jesus. We are more spirited than spiritual.

4. *The Grace of God*

One phase of the Kingdom which John missed is Christ's
revelation of God's forgiving grace. John lived before
the last act was staged in the divine drama of deliverance.
John had preached repentance but he had not fathomed
the depths of divine forgiveness as plumbed by the cross.
He glimpsed a God who would punish the unrepentant but
he had not comprehended a heavenly Father who was
watching for the returning prodigal afar off and would run

[25] Cf. Evelyn Underhill: *The Life of the Spirit*, Methuen & Co., London, p. 24.
[26] Matthew 11:12.

forth to meet him, to say nothing of the God who "so loved the world that he gave his only begotten Son, that whosoever believeth in him should not perish, but have everlasting life." [27]

John might have understood Jesus' words, "Greater love hath no man than this, that a man lay down his life for his friends," [28] for that, in a sense, is what he himself did; but could he have grasped Jesus' inclusive interpretation of the friends for whom he would die? Jesus did not die merely for the friends of his own circle or nation. Jesus died for those who despised him, for those who never knew him, for those who were not yet born out of every land and tongue and kindred. Jesus died for all men. And in so doing he uttered love's most magnanimous word: "Father, forgive them for they know not what they do." [29]

John sought to bring the self-sufficient and rebellious to repentance; but could he have understood the post-Calvary words of Robert Louis Stevenson, also addressed to the conceited and self-sufficient: "Why not the grace of your Maker and Redeemer? He who died for you, He who upholds you, He whom you daily crucify afresh? There is nothing but God's grace. We walk upon it; we breathe it; we live and die by it: it makes the nails and axles of the universe; and a puppy in pajamas prefers self-conceit." [30]

We have seen Calvary, the symbol of God's forgiving grace. But how effective are we in preaching sermons on the forgiveness of sins? A survey of contemporary sermons reveals every verbal device for ferreting out sins, for showing up social sins, for denouncing sins, but alas, not very much light on the divine forgiveness of sins. God's *for-*

[27] John 3:16.
[28] *Ibid.*, 15:13.
[29] Luke 23:34.
[30] Robert Louis Stevenson, *The Ebb Tide,* Grosset & Dunlap, p. 170.

giving grace is one of the nearly forgotten notes in present-day preaching.

If we are to revive the note of God's forgiving grace, we must first reappreciate the fulness of God's *giving grace*. To do this we must go beyond the court-room terminology of the older evangelism and also beyond the laboratory language of the latter-day scientific age. Under the shadow of the prestige accorded to science in recent years, we have stressed the laws of God and overlooked the grace of God.

Even nature reveals to deeper gaze something more than the mechanical rigidities of iron law. As Sir James Jeans reminds us, phases of our physical world parallel music more than mathematics. There are lovely overtones and rich flourishes in nature. There are extras which do not seem strictly required by natural law. Take sunsets, for instance. By scientific measurements we can predict the exact moment of the sun's setting at a given place. But who can foretell the colors of that sunset? This evening the western horizon may be adorned in gorgeous red; to-morrow night the decoration may be a purple robe flecked with gold. These rich colorings do not seem absolutely necessary to the operation of nature's laws or the practical uses of man. All that man's physical needs and health would have required is the alternation of light and darkness. But the Creator throws in the sunset colors as extras. The wild flowers which "waste their sweetness on the desert air" and blanket with beauty the rutted battlefields once drenched with blood—they are not needed for food. Nature has grace as well as law.

And when we turn from nature to human nature, we see the destruction and depravity of man. From some angles it might be argued that man is becoming more brutal. In the battle of Hastings William conquered Harold with ten

thousand men. In such a struggle there were opportunities
for individual chivalry and mercy. But on the war fronts
of 1942, war has been dehumanized until casualties are
counted in tanks, planes and ships while the millions of
broken bodies are treated as almost incidental. Nevertheless, organized brutalities cannot blind us to the good Sa-
maritanism which spreads amid the cruelties. A critic said
of the late James M. Barrie that he rattled the cans when he
brought around the milk of human kindness. But with all
our noisy and sometimes too apparent efforts at doing good,
and despite the insincere motives and sentimental shallow-
ness often to be found in our philanthropy, the milk of
human kindness is growing in supply. There are more and
more strong persons willing to bear the burdens of the weak
and more and more levers for lifting the fallen.

We are the heirs of grace. When childhood is normal,
none of us pays his way to maturity. Those sleepless nights
of mothers, those anxious hours of fathers, are rarely fully
paid for; although such is the grace inherent in love that
parents get their pay in the sweetness of the sacrifice itself.
But that does not lessen the child's indebtedness for the unmerited favors received. We are started on the voyage of
life by the tugs of parental love, as a ship is nosed out of
dock by the little boats before its own propellers begin to
turn. Then we get under our own steam and sail away, all
too often forgetting to pay adequately those who started
us. And on the voyage we are aided by friends, enriched
by inherited wisdom, safeguarded by institutions, protected
in our privileges—all of them services for which we did not
pay. Society with all its sinfulness is ingrained with grace.

In our law-conscious and tax-conscious generation we
need to stress repeatedly this unpayable indebtedness.
There are not only the ne'er-do-wells who think the world

owes them a living, and the thoughtless folk who take their privileges for granted, but there are the successful persons who with their charities and taxes assume that they are more than paying their own way. The human race could be roughly divided into those who feel that they are giving more than they get and those who feel that they are getting more than they give. The former are restless and discontented, no matter what they have; the latter have a spirit of gratitude and a peace of mind with whatever they have. It makes a fundamental difference whether a person lives in this world with a creditor complex or a debtor complex. If we look around at our fellows, it is easy to see those who make us feel that we are doing more than our share. But when we lift our eyes to see all the places where the shadow of the cross has fallen, we exclaim with Paul, "Where sin abounded, grace did much more abound," [31] and we sing with Isaac Watts:

> Were the whole realm of nature mine,
> That were a present far too small;
> Love so amazing, so divine,
> Demands my soul, my life, my all.

Such a humbling sense of gratitude mellows us into repentance. The mere recognition of our sins does not necessarily beget the mood of repentance. It may only stir bitter remorse, or start a defense of alibis, or end in humiliation rather than humility, or result in social comparisons which generate a clubbable atmosphere of mutual exoneration. To make us truly repentant our sins must be set in the light of the love that has been injured and the grace that has been spurned. It is the grace of godliness as seen in the person of Jesus Christ that softens thick-skinned self-assurance

[31] Romans 5:20.

into sensitive self-criticism and then goes on to transmute humiliation, which is self-centered, into trustful humility, which is God-centered.

Moreover, the sense of God's gracious forgiveness of our unpayable indebtedness is the stimulant essential to produce a forgiving mood toward our fellows. Recognizing this, Jesus linked our prayer for forgiveness with our promise to forgive. "Forgive us our debts, as we forgive our debtors." To forgive is as difficult as to repent. For both, we need an encompassing love. Forgiveness means remitting the right to retaliate, plus erasing the feeling of resentment, plus the reinstatement of the wrongdoer in the old relationship of good-will. When a person says, "I can forgive but I cannot forget," the process of forgiveness is not finished. Nor is it enough to say, "I shall forgive and forget, but we can never be the same again." Forgiveness never reaches the fulness of stature as it was manifest in Christ Jesus our Lord until it becomes complete reconciliation. And for that we need divine grace.

Life is not so simple that we can dismiss a wrongdoing by saying, "Let bygones be bygones." There are really no bygones in character's career. Our past remains a part of us. In this fact lie both the seriousness of our sinful acts and also the hope of forgiving them. Because my past is still a part of me, I can still repair it. Because the injury which I have done another is still being carried somewhere in his personality, there is still a chance of paying the debt. The strands of time have not slipped through our fingers; they have been woven into the fabric of our personalities. Were we to have seen the Prodigal twenty years after his return, we would have noted the scars of his sin for his Father's forgiveness did not remove those, but we would also have observed that the reconciliation had enriched his relationship with his Father.

The cocksureness of his early smartness would have been converted into the modesty of wisdom, and humble gratitude for his Father's goodness would have made him magnanimous toward his elder brother's selfishness. The memories of his early lovelessness would, as in Paul's case, have deepened the quality of his love.

A deaf and dumb person when asked, "What is forgiveness?" took a pencil and wrote: "It is the odor which flowers give when trampled upon." With such fragrance Christ fills the situations where his forgiving love is revealed.

Furthermore, God's grace is not only forgiving but also *empowering* and *sustaining*. And the Baptist failed to plumb this latter aspect also. The contrast between John and Jesus at this point is somewhat like that between an inexperienced and an experienced swimmer. John's activity resembles the actions of one who is just learning to swim. Such a person seems to feel that he must do it all himself. He beats the water furiously, splashing and gasping. Contrast his excited action with that of the experienced swimmer who trusts the buoyancy of the water and with lithe grace gives himself to its sustaining support. Jesus, if we may put it so, was like a graceful swimmer in the waters of life.

Yes, there is an empowering and sustaining grace which John did not know. Do we? Joseph Fort Newton reports a conversation with a British soldier concerning a sermon: "A British Tommy gave me a synopsis of the sermon, and I can still see his big blue eyes and hear his soft voice as he told me, point by point, what the preacher had said. The subject was 'The Grace of God,' and Tommy closed his account with exquisite courtesy in these words: 'The minister told us that the grace of God is plentiful, sufficient for all need, and near at hand, but he did not tell us what the grace of God is; perhaps you, sir, will be good enough to do that.' " [32]

The word "grace" like the term "glory," "Kingdom" and their ilk have been jingling about in our ecclesiastical vocabularies, until, like coins long carried in the pocket, they have worn almost too smooth to pass current. But the term "grace" was recently reminted in fresh and simple form by Henry Nelson Wieman. Professor Wieman confessed that during the last ten years his mind has swung to a revived interest in the grace of God. He says: "The grace of God is the good which God puts into each concrete situation over and above all that man can do or plan or even imagine." [33] If I were to change that definition in any regard, it would be to add the word "deserve." It is the good over and above all that man can do or plan or imagine or deserve. It is immeasurable, unmerited favor.

"It has been said lately that men as a rule do not care much about the doctrine of grace until they reach the age of thirty." [34] The age limit set in that remark reminds me of the statement of a young Boston lawyer. Some years ago a publisher suggested the need of a book on the period of the thirties. He said that there had been a plethora of books on youth and a deluge of treatises on all the things that "begin at forty"; but nothing on the years in-between. Shortly after that suggestion was made I was lunching with a group of young professional men, and I raised the question as to what are the significant characteristics of the years between thirty and forty. One comment lingers in my memory. Said a young attorney: "It is in the thirties

[32] Joseph Fort Newton: *The New Preaching*, Cokesbury, p. 120.
[33] *The Christian Century*, January 25, 1939, p. 117.
[34] T. R. Glover: *The Nature and Purpose of a Christian Society*, G. H. Doran & Co., p. 34.

that a man learns to accept his limitations without losing respect for himself and faith in his future." He went on: "I know now that I shall not make a fortune at the bar but I still am thrilled by the practice of law."

In the thirties when the period of adjustment merges into the "period of achievement," when he must learn to fortify himself against life's frustrations, when he begins to feel responsibility for the young lives which lean upon him and look to him for guidance, it is then that a man should grope for the One "able to do exceeding abundantly above all that we ask or think, according to the power that worketh in us." [35] But whatever groping they may do for the divine grace in their mystical moments, the men of the thirties and forties seem less open to cooperation with the "power not ourselves" than during the periods before and after. "Your old men shall dream dreams, your young men shall see visions"; [36] but your middle-aged seem to miss the divine visitation. Immersion in the material struggle, self-assurance which mounts with achievement, spiritual and sometimes mental sclerosis which impedes the free flow of unaccustomed ideas and the fair facing of uncongenial facts—these and other factors like them make the middle years life's most dangerous age, at least from the religious standpoint.

And the peril of this unspirituality is heightened by the fact that it comes at the period of most power. If we were to retain the spiritual sensitivity and social idealism of early youth when we reach the age which puts us in charge of industry, institutions and government, truly the vicious circles of recurring evils, even of war, would be checked. Except the middle-aged be converted and become as little

[35] Ephesians 3:20.
[36] Joel 2:28.

children, the Kingdom of Heaven will not spread far as a social reality.

It is nothing less than a tragedy that the note of divine grace is muted through our younger and middle years. The benighted modern man who trusts only in human efficiency and the scheme of law, who is so enamored of the scientific method that he sneers at anything which outdistances reason, who counts as real only those forces which can be computed in statistics—that man is missing "the life which is life indeed." If there is one doctrine above others which young ministers should study and stress during the next decade, it is that of *divine grace*.

But, alas, there are preachers who run their parishes as if there were no Holy Spirit.

5. *The Force We Forget*

The old question which Paul put to the church at Ephesus bids us pause: "Have ye received the Holy Ghost since ye believed?" [37] We cannot make the answer which they gave, for the Ephesians replied: "We have not so much as heard whether there be any Holy Ghost." Paul asked, "Unto what then were ye baptized?" and they answered, "Unto John's baptism." Then said Paul: "John verily baptized with the baptism of repentance, saying unto the people that they should believe on him which should come after him, that is, on Christ Jesus." But we are they who have been baptized with Christian baptism "into the name of the Father, and of the Son, and of the Holy Ghost." But what shall we say when the question confronts us, "Have ye received the Holy Ghost since ye believed?"

What is it to receive the Holy Spirit? Let us approach

[37] Acts 19:2.

the process by a few simple though crude parallels. A boy goes to college. At first the campus is unfamiliar and the curriculum uncongenial. He attends classes, he obeys the rules, many of which seem to him meaningless. The whole procedure strikes him as rather pointless. But after a time light begins to break on his mind. Organizations take him in. He comes to feel himself a part of the school. He begins to see what it is all about. Its enthusiasms and traditions lay hold on him. We say, "He has caught the spirit of the school." And with that there comes an awakened interest, a lift, a new birth of enthusiasm.

The same process may be seen in a church. A person joins a parish but he does not at first feel a part of it. He attends the services and listens to the sermons. He may float along on the current of the church's activities and yet he does not quite feel himself "in the swim." Then after a time he begins to be a factor in the parish life. The loyalty of the people becomes understandable and contagious. The point of the whole proceeding becomes apparent to him. In short, he catches the spirit of the church. Then to him there comes a buoyancy in the service, a new birth of insight and inspiration.

Similarly men catch the spirit of a person as well as of a place. John Buchan in *Pilgrim's Way* tells how his young mind was fired by his great teacher, Gilbert Murray, from whom he caught his passion for the classics and through whom he experienced a new birth of intellectual interest.

All this is, of course, a most inadequate parallel to what is meant by receiving the Holy Spirit. Yet it is a parallel. Watch the disciples after the death of Jesus. They were stunned. They could not comprehend the collapse of their enterprise and their hopes. They went about their routine duties in a fog. But they held on and held together. They nourished the memories of their comradeship with Christ. They communed with their invisible Leader in their hours of meditation. They waited in expectant mood for his return. And most of all they were bringing their wills into a state of surrender to their Lord's will when it should be revealed. And then at Pentecost when they were all together in one place, the light broke. The One whom they had not comprehended in the days of his flesh became clearer to them. They caught his spirit in a new reality, and were caught up by his spirit. There came to them a new exaltation of their hopes, a new quickening of the pulse, an enduement of power from on high.

And like the apostles at Pentecost, Christians since that time have testified to the witness of the Spirit. But have we received the Holy Spirit? When we read and hear about the power from above, are we like deaf persons at a concert who finger their programmes and clap with the crowd but whose smiles are sicklied over with the pale cast of pretense? Augustine Birrell, writing of the Brontë sisters, says that of the three brilliant daughters of the Yorkshire rectory Anne alone had "enough religion to give her pleasure." Many persons have enough religion to make them feel *uncomfortable when they do wrong but not enough to make them feel good when they do right*. But there can come a stage in religion, as in the study of music, when what we have been trying to get, gets us; when, because we have learned to like what he likes and to comprehend what he taught, the Master can say to us, "Henceforth I call you not servants; for the servant knoweth not what his lord doeth; but I have called you friends." [38] Duty has been transformed into desire; religion has become a lift rather than a load; God has emerged from the void as a living God.

[38] John 15:15.

When that stage is reached, we know what it is to receive the Holy Spirit.

Having glanced at the parallels, let us look a little more in detail at the process of reaching that stage wherein religion comes alive through the witness of the Spirit. In this we recognize differences of temperament as well as diversities of gifts. There are those who live in deeds not words, those whose approach to the throne of grace is by the plodding steps of duty well, if perhaps laboriously, done. There are others so sensitive to the invisibles that they catch their intimations afar off and their friends think them possessed of psychic power. The matter-of-fact and the mystical travel toward the Holy of Holies by different roads. But allowing for these differences, we may designate certain steps essential to the entrance of the Holy Spirit.

First, is the *emptying of self*. The world is too much with us and within us. The things of sense are so readily at hand. The slopes of earthly living seem so to lie that they pour their drains into our mental reservoirs. The gravity of competitive life is toward self-centeredness. Thus we fill up with superficialities until deep no longer calleth unto deep.

Many are so filled with their own interests, their self-importance, their self-sufficiency that they view no situation objectively but only through the lens of their own self-interest. Eyes have they, but they see not. The only conversation to which they really listen is the echo of their own opinions. The only music they genuinely enjoy is the blowing of their own horns. Ears have they, but they hear not. "Woe unto you that are full!" [39] said Jesus, for he experienced the futility of trying to get his message into minds surfeited with their own conceits.

[39] Luke 6:25.

As an airplane seeks to find a hole in the clouds for a landing, so God looks for an opening through the low ceiling of earth-bound spirits. Viewed from the divine side, these opportunities for deep calling unto deep are what the Quakers called "openings"; viewed from the human side, they mean an emptying of the spirit.

Sometimes this emptying of the self is induced by dramatic or tragic circumstances. Calamity, disaster, the death of a loved one, can bowl us over and leave us as empty as an overturned cup. We see then how weak is our self-sufficiency, how worthless the baubles of our Vanity Fair. The function of religious faith at such a moment is to see that the trouble humbles us rather than humiliates us. If we remain self-centered, then calamity only serves to humiliate us; if we become God-centered, lost in the larger results, then disaster produces humility, the basic requirement for receiving the Holy Spirit. Such was the transformation which took place in Job. The voice out of the whirlwind humbled the sufferer's defiant spirit. Faced with the immensity of the universe, Job realized that there are limits to man's rationalizing, that we cannot find where the cloud of sorrow starts, that all our boasted knowledge is but an island in the vast ocean of mystery, and as the island of knowledge grows larger, the shore line of mystery becomes longer. At the end of his wits, he surrendered in trust to a Higher Wisdom. Having clung to his trust, "Though he slay me, yet will I trust in him," [40] Job comes through until in a burst of luminous insight he cries: "I have heard of thee by the hearing of the ear; but now mine eye seeth thee." [41]

Or this emptying of the self may be induced by entering

[40] Job 13:15.
[41] *Ibid.*, 42:5.

into the sufferings of others. Some time ago a woman expressed a rather common attitude in her remark that she did not wish to hear about the war, to witness tragic plays or to see things which would work on her sympathies, because she had sufficient troubles of her own. Such a comment is a pretty clear revelation of a mind in need of being delivered from its own self-interests. There is a difference between borrowing trouble and sharing sorrow. And here again it is a question of egocentricity. When we are self-centered, every trouble taken on seems an added burden. When we are freed from our egocentricity, the entrance into others' sorrows is an exit for our own anxieties. The mental health of a person can be measured by the extent to which his interests move in circles beyond himself. Knowing what a purgatory men make for themselves by their self-centeredness, Gerald Heard has defined hell as "a place composed of completely egoistic persons." And his statement is in line with the *Theologia Germanica* which asserts that "nothing burns in hell but the ego."

When one has become accustomed to being a star performer, it is hard to stay off the center of the stage. This weakness is to be seen not only in the consummate egoists who have been spoiled by public flattery, but also in miserable little creatures whose obscure stage of action may be on some side street. We need to get out of ourselves by getting into the lives of others. The Holy Spirit dwells with those of a humble and contrite heart, whose humility consists not in thinking meanly of themselves but in not thinking of themselves at all.

Or the emptying of the self may "begin in a sort of restlessness, a feeling that there is something more in existence, some absolute meaning, some more searching obligation, that we have not reached." [42] The seeming fulness of our living is so deceptive. Just as a little water in the bottom of a glass may be shaken until it slops over, so we may churn the meager contents of our lives until they too spill over and cause us to think that we are living the full life. How common is the spectacle of the overactive and underfed spirits. But when we stop to think and give the contents of our minds a chance to settle, we discover how far we are from the fulness of Him who came that we might have life and have it abundantly. The slightest incident may serve to induce the stillness which reveals our emptiness. It was only a darkling thrush that opened the great heart of Thomas Hardy to glimpse the cavity in his own confidence.

> So little cause for carolings
> Of such ecstatic sound
> Was written on terrestrial things
> Afar or nigh around,
> That I could think there trembled through
> His happy goodnight air,
> Some blessed Hope whereof he knew
> And I was unaware.[43]

When we hear courageous spirits singing in the face of approaching storm; when we see serene faces smiling in the shadow of approaching death; when we see sturdy souls bearing up under burdens which would break our backs and hearts, then we realize there is a Reality beyond the human and the natural. Our spirits become humble with the sense of our own inadequacy and penitent at the pettiness of our living.

[42] Evelyn Underhill: *The Life of the Spirit*, Methuen & Co., London, p. 213.
[43] *The Darkling Thrush.*

Or it may be the magnifying of individual traits through crowd demonstrations that reveals the turbulent churning of our shallow lives. In July, 1940, it was my privilege to be in Mexico City on the day of the national election. From our hotel window I watched the milling crowds of partisans, swirling through the Zocala, repeatedly broken up by the police and then ever reforming. Above the shouting and the shooting loomed the two-century old towers of the Cathedral and beyond in the distance could be seen the snow-clad peaks of the extinct volcanoes, Popocatapetl and Iztaccihuatl. It was a most vivid contrast between the volatile and the stable, between the furious passion of the moment and the quiet strength of the eternal. As I looked from the snows of the mountains to the noisy crowds, I felt like saying with Emerson, "Why so hot, little man?"

After the emptying of the self, comes the *opening of the spirit*. "Behold I stand at the door and knock; if any man hear my voice and open the door, I will come in to him and will sup with him, and he with me." [44] The door must be opened from the inside. As Holman Hunt correctly pointed out, there is no latch on the side of the Divine Spirit, although he yearns for entrance.

As in the emptying of the self, so in the opening of the spirit, the process may be dramatically or suddenly induced. To a young courtier at the Jerusalem court, religion had been a kind of graceful and formal adjunct to his service of the king. Life moved smoothly for his favored circle and fairly so for the country at large because a strong ruler was on the throne. Then a blow fell. The strong King Uzziah was stricken. That break was the occasion through which God became real to the young attendant Isaiah. "In the year that King Uzziah died I saw also the Lord sitting upon

[44] Revelation 3:10.

a throne," [45] he writes. The death of a king in whom he had trusted led Isaiah to realize the sovereignty of a Divine King who dieth not. God moved in from the circumference of Isaiah's world to the center. And in surrendering to the Lord as sovereign, Isaiah opened his spirit to the Living God.

But is deep to call to deep only when disaster or dramatic developments topple us into the depths? To treat our spirits thus is as stupid as to let our radios remain silent until they are needed to send S O S calls. God is a very present help in time of trouble, but he is best found to be so by those who have learned to communicate with him when no emergency is on. We must cultivate the practice of the presence of God for the sake of his companionship and not merely of his succor.

Toward this end *quiescence* is a first requisite. The mind must be "recollected," as the mystics say, until the hum of the world fades from consciousness. The body should be relaxed, and the condition should be one of complete mental and bodily rest. Yet it is "a rest most busy" as one seer has expressed it. For the state of surrendered quiet must be supplemented by a second requisite: *attention*. The quieted mind must receive and hold the idea which it desires to realize; and this idea must be real for it, so that attention is concentrated on it spontaneously. The more completely the idea absorbs the mind, the greater its transforming power. Such attention must be cultivated, and for most of us requires external help. Hence the value of vocal prayer, altars, private prayer rooms and other aids to worship. At this point a word should be said about the use of silence in our church services. Nothing is more imperative, and yet periods of silence need to be safeguarded against

[45] Isaiah 6:1.

the danger of spiritual emptiness. Limited in number is "the aristocracy of the attentive" that can make a moving experience out of a Quaker meeting. The conventional "silent prayer" of an ordinary congregation may easily lapse into a superficial introspection, or worse, into that "wandering of mind and coldness of heart" preparatory to putting on the coats and resuming the secular concerns. The utilization of silence must include the training of attention. Toward that end may be suggested frequent use of directed petitions with short intervals for silent contemplation of specific objectives.

And the third element in opening the mind to spiritual suggestion is: *feeling*. When an idea is charged with emotion, it is far more likely to be realized. The old revivals with their corporate and contagious enthusiasm had a popular emotional suggestibility not generated by what we call "dignified services." Our conventional church services lack emotion and the eccentric popular religious movements are capitalizing that omission. We may deplore the intellectual vacuity of those messages which attract large Sunday night crowds of rather shallow minds. But we who pride ourselves on preaching to thoughtful congregations overestimate the capacity of the intellect in appropriating spiritual power. A recent reading of the late Thomas Wolfe's autobiographical books revealed how he immersed all his physical senses in the common experiences of life, absorbing sensations at every pore. What new possibilities he uncovered in the most commonplace acts! In comparison with the torrent of sensations which surged through Thomas Wolfe, what a trickling stream of experiences do our senses yield us! Now the saints, whom the church honors as the great mystics, were those who opened all their senses to things unseen and eternal. As one has said: "The saints are neither special creations nor spiritual freaks, but those who have learned St. Augustine's aspiration: 'My life shall be a real life, being wholly full of Thee.' " [46] We must get God into our Unconscious. Religion remains vague to a person until it gets into his dreams. We dream about persons we love: we should dream about the God we love.

These openings of the mind through *quiescence, attention,* and *feeling* are only opportunities for the Holy Spirit. His entrance depends on what we do with these open doors. Here religion advances beyond psychology. We are indebted to the psychologists for showing us the mind's moments of greatest suggestibility. We know now that entrance to the mind is easiest just after waking before the mental shutters have been closed for the day's defensive living, and just before slipping into slumber when the censorship is again relaxed. But these valuable moments must be utilized for something more than the vapid, and false, formula of Mr. Coué, "Day by day in every way we are getting better and better." There is a vital difference between meditating on oneself and adoring a transcendent God. A little exercise which I have found helpful in starting the day is this: before I rise from the bed or take up the paper with its welter of world interests, I say aloud to myself some things about God—oh, any sayings which come into my mind, such as "God is Love"; "From everlasting to everlasting thou art God";—just sayings which swim spontaneously into my mind. The list, I discover, grows with daily use. I find too that in framing these words aloud I help to focus my attention and pull myself together.

[46] Evelyn Underhill: *Concerning the Inner Life*, E. P. Dutton & Co., p. 121.

It is like the poise of a diver before leaping into the current of the day's distractions.

Muriel Lester has suggested the value of looking into the dark at the dead of the night, and thinking about God, when, for instance, she finds herself lying awake at two or three o'clock in the morning. In the inky darkness, the physical surroundings and the self's belongings are blotted out, and one's thoughts can dwell without distraction on the vastness of God. And thus suggested methods might be multiplied. The development of these interludes of private devotion is increasingly imperative as the crowded schedules disrupt the traditional habits of church-going and send people scurrying into quietudes for longer and longer week-ends.

But the religion adequate for our day must be more than "what a man does with his own solitariness." "We wrestle not against principalities, against powers, against the rulers of darkness of this world, against spiritual wickedness in high places." [47] Our real enemy in the present issue with Germany is not Hans and Fritz, but the spirit of hate and greed and fear which has caught Hans and Fritz and many others with them. There is a devilish, a sort of demonic, spirit abroad in the world. The atmosphere is charged with it. To fight that spirit, the sons of God must unloose a spirit, for only spirit can defeat spirit, only light can drive out darkness. The destructiveness of this demonic spirit now raging through the world did not rise from men's solitary speculations. It was fomented by fellowship and organized into action. Likewise the spirit of grace, if it is to abound over the spirit of sin, must not be left to solitary cultivation. Our world needs a Pentecost more than monastic cells.

[47] Ephesians 6:12.

6. *The Charmed Circle*

The testimony of experience is that the presence of fellowseekers helps to make the divine presence more real. There are times, of course, when this is not true. I have moods wherein I feel that to go off alone into some lovely wood or by the restful sea brings me closer to God than to mingle with men in public worship. And there is a place for solitude. The religious man's direct experience of God is like the artist's lonely and intense apprehension of beauty or the poet's solitary dream. But these lonely flashes of luminous insight do not give me a sufficiently steady light to live by, any more than the glow of the fireflies on a summer night or the flashes of lightning in a storm shed sufficient light to read by. Left to myself, my moods fluctuate. There come hours of exultant faith wherein I feel convinced of God's goodness. There come moments of mystic insight when the atmosphere clears and the very foothills of heaven are visible.

But I also have dark moods when I dwell in the basement of my nature and take low views of my environment. I have cynical hours when I discount the motives of my fellowmen and lose faith in noble causes. These high and low tides of the spirit surge in upon me; and in the handling of them I need the help of others. My private spiritual exercises meet somewhat the same difficulties as do those physical setting-up exercises which I start every now and then in my room. At least every New Year's Day I resolve to follow regular physical exercises immediately after rising. My good resolutions in this regard usually last until the first severe cold snap. Private physical drills lack the incentive for continuance and the value for mental release which are to be found in a game or a walk with friends. Likewise in spiritual exercises, we need fellowship to make them continuous and effective. While we have no means of accurate observation, we hazard the guess that those who neglect the assemblies of public worship are not as a general rule very faithful in their private devotions.

Furthermore in dark times such as the present, it is not good for the God-seeker to be shut off from his fellow searchers. It is so easy to fall into Elijah's mood and say, "And I, even I only, am left." We that do truly and earnestly seek the Lord need to be heartened by seeing how many others have not bowed the knee to Baal. In our dangerous darkness of a world at war, lonely picket duty is likely to sap one's courage. When the secular order is tragically divisive, we doubly need the sense of spiritual solidarity which comes through Christ and reaches beyond national boundaries.

Moreover, the presence of fellow seekers not only makes God more real through the contagion of their faith but also through the discipline imposed in adjusting ourselves to their differences. An interpreter of Bach has pointed out that one of the factors which gave his music a peculiarly appealing quality was the fact that Bach composed usually at home. He wrote for various members of a large family circle. And he often had to write in, or within sound of the kitchen, where pots and pans were being scoured and occasionally dropped, where his numerous children were running in and out. Bach did not have to be sheltered, segregated, aloof in order to catch his inspiration. And the seeker after the Divine Spirit who feels that he must get away from men in order to get near to God should search his heart, lest there be some antisocial motives lurking under cover of a spurious spirituality. "If a man say, I love God, and hatest his brother, he is a liar; for he that loveth not his brother whom he hath seen, how can he love God whom he hath not seen?" [48]

The world is not much helped by those "saints" who have to be kept sealed in solitude in order to keep them sweet, nor by the folk who can worship God only in congenial surroundings with "the right people." It makes for the vitality of our faith and the vividness of our mystic insights to meet in Christ's name with persons of unequal abilities and differing economic and social backgrounds. In our services of worship we should seek to combine thought and symbol, message and ritual into a medium so universally understandable that "elephants can wade and fish can swim." When we gather together in the name of him in whom there is neither bond nor free, male nor female, east nor west, the blending makes for that brotherhood which is the essential basis for the true worship of God.

This fellowship in worship makes also for that cooperation in service, whereby concern for the Kingdom becomes commitment to its tasks. "Where two or three are gathered together in my name, there am I in the midst of them." [49] Fellowship opens the way for the Christ Spirit and also furthers the following of him. It is the charmed circle in which the kingdom that is within us reaches out toward the realization of the kingdom that is to come "on earth as it is in heaven."

[48] I John 4:20.
[49] Matthew 18:20.

THE CHILDREN OF WISDOM
VS.
THE CHILDREN OF THE MARKET PLACE

Whereunto then shall I liken the men of this generation? and to what are they like? They are like unto children sitting in the market place, and calling one to another, and saying, We have piped unto you, and ye have not danced; we have mourned to you, and ye have not wept. For John the Baptist came neither eating bread nor drinking wine; and ye say, He hath a devil. The Son of Man is come eating and drinking; and ye say, Behold a gluttonous man, and a wine-bibber, a friend of publicans and sinners! But wisdom is justified of all her children.

LUKE 7:31-5.

Wisdom is not finally tested in the schools,
Wisdom cannot be passed from one having it
    to another not having it,
Wisdom is of the soul, is not susceptible of
    proof, is its own proof.
WALT WHITMAN, *Song of the
                    Open Road*

THE CHILDREN OF WISDOM
VS.
THE CHILDREN OF THE MARKET PLACE

What a trenchant description did Jesus give of those sideline spectators who tried the patience of John and Jesus! Children of the market place calling the tunes for the messengers of God, expecting those messengers to be minstrels ready to please their patrons! When the Baptist appeared along the Jordan, they flocked out to hear him. He was a new sensation, an interesting phenomenon, one of the old prophets reproduced. His strong language and stern manner were no doubt pleasing at first, for listeners rather like to hear preachers call them "offspring of vipers" and other salty terms, as long as it is *in broad general fashion*. People rather like pulpit browbeating en masse. It is when you start singling out specific sins with rifle practice that pews begin to empty. When John began to drive his ascetic demands home, they turned away, saying he had a devil.

Then Jesus came. Again he was something new. His pungent parables, his healing power, his manner of authority drew great crowds. To hear him was "the thing to do." Here was a leader to kindle the fires of patriotic anger against Rome. Here was one who should set himself apart in Messianic aloofness. But he went on dining with publicans and sinners, mingling with men in their daily routines. They wanted Jesus to demonstrate his divine mission with more drastic and denunciatory methods, even with a crown. When he refused they turned away.

Neither John nor Jesus would join in the tunes the children of the market place called.

1. *The Pipers*

How clearly we see contemporary moods mirrored in those Palestinian crowds. Consider the pipers who desire God's messengers to dance to their tunes. The modern cult of comfort has invaded the precincts of religion. Our schedule of living has been arranged somewhat as the Harvard student said that he had adjusted his courses for the semester, when he said to his room-mate after signing up, "I am lucky this term. I haven't a class before ten o'clock in the morning, or up more than one flight of stairs." In order to make religion appeal to our comfort-loving contemporaries, we have cushioned our pews, softened our lights, shortened our sermons, adjusted our hours of service to interfere as little as possible with the other activities of our pleasure-loving parishioners. No doubt we shall soon be air-conditioning our churches and some enterprising pastor will ere long advertise his sanctuary as "the coolest spot in town." More than this, we have watered down the moral demands in order to make our spiritual medicine as palatable as possible. We have tried to secure harmony through comfort rather than through the traditional Christian method of sacrifice. When the general attitude is thus patterned, the preaching of the cross is not very realistic. At a recent noon-day Lenten service, the song leader told the congregation to make themselves comfortable and remain seated while they sang, for he knew they were tired. Then he announced "The Old Rugged Cross."

The invitation of Christ was negatived in the last half century by a revival of Rousseau's return to nature, popularized by the Freudian psychology. Under this influence the impression spread that any considerable repression of man's instinctive tendencies is liable to produce pathological conditions and is therefore an evil. Along with this Freudian emphasis, went a hedonistic philosophy which exalts personal pleasure and interprets it almost exclusively in sensuous terms. Professor Sorokin has called our civilization a "sensate culture" because it is mainly directed toward sense-satisfaction. Comfort, social security and personal pleasure have been the prevailing objectives. "We have quietly closed our eyes to the eternal Substance of things and opened them only to the shows and shams of things." [1] Enlightened egoism has been proclaimed as the sufficient guide, both for individuals and groups.

In this general atmosphere, the health and happiness cults have sprung up like green bay trees. The effect of these movements upon contemporary religion has not yet been fully measured, for the end is not yet. In the early stage of my ministry Mr. Coué, the French cultist, visited our country and captured a host of devotees with his delightful formula, "Day by day in every way I am getting better and better." In the glow of his popularity, I delivered a series of Sunday night sermons on the relation of religion to the new psychology. (I feel that I should apologize to someone for those sermons today. I would not have to apologize to very many because I preached them on Sunday nights.) Who would be so inane as to use Coué's formula in these frightful days? And yet many a minister is

[1] Thomas Carlyle: *Past and Present*, Book III, Chap. I.

making some curious combinations of Couéism and the cross. Their religion is success psychology tinged with evangelism. In general their sermons are delightful homilies on the art of successful self-management, immune from the germs of social ills and devoid of divine remedies. They sweeten the bread of life into dessert. They omit the notes of man's depravity and God's judgment.

This easy-going philosophy is an atmosphere too enervating for personal or social regeneration. "In such an atmosphere societies are bound to have more luxury, more vice, and even more crime. Now we can see why sport and war still remain the main recreations of modern nations, for there is a close connection between the false philosophies which we have just discussed and the fact that human beings continually fluctuate between being playboys or soldiers." [2]

2. *The Mourners*

And now the ecclesiastical climate has changed. In this winter of the world's discontent, the children of the market place are calling a different tune. They have shifted from the dance to the dirge. Whereas in the glittering 1920's we were marching gaily to Zion as if on parade, we seem now to be, theologically speaking, in a retreat, a veritable rout back to the mood of defeat. Man is now seen as a pitiful victim of an inner pervasive evil power which he frequently loathes and opposes, but cannot overcome. Those who most eloquently preach this triumph of sin are a younger group who lean to the left on social issues while they insist with Augustinian emphasis on man's spiritual helplessness. The sternness of the old evangelical preach-

[2] Charles A. Ellwood: *The World's Need of Christ*, Abingdon Cokesbury, p. 42.

ing has been revived but with less optimism, because our social gospel has shifted our focus to the group, and the difficulties of redeeming group life grow more apparent. Disillusionment has destroyed "the faith in man and his highest values as the clue to the nature of God."

The swing to realism represents a healthy corrective to the comfortable Utopianism which preceded it. James Truslow Adams tells us that the spell which Emerson cast over his youthful mind is not recoverable now in his maturity, and he explains this fact by saying that Emerson lacked a sense of the tragedy of life. The gentle transcendentalism of Concord is hardly adequate to confront the totalitarianism of today's world. No philosophy which lacks the sense of tragedy can satisfy us. The church must recognize man's natural depravity and absolute need of divine grace.

Yet there is danger that the dust-and-ashes mood may become a deadly sort of new orthodoxy. In the current vogue of denouncing liberalism, its critics should distinguish between the genuine article and the comfortable counterfeits which carried its label. *Real liberalism* should survive to keep alive faith in man's free thought, to respect the power of reason to find clues to God, and to keep healthy the nerves of social passion. True liberals never counted on being "carried to the skies on flowery beds of ease." To depend on heavenward transportation is likely to be disappointing whether the conveyance be a Barthian cataclysm or a humanistic escalator.

Furthermore realism should not be made completely synonymous with pessimism. Some of our so-called realists are so submerged in their pessimism that they get only a submarine outlook, from which they see merely something to be blown up. The view from the periscope of a submarine is not necessarily more realistic than that from the bridge of a liner. The difference is in the range and the horizon. When Paul took a periscopic view of his inner state, he cried, "O wretched man that I am! Who shall deliver me from the body of this death." [3] But when he swept the horizon of history he cried, "Where sin abounded grace did much more abound." [4] Both views were realistic.

And in deflating man's overweening confidence in himself care must be taken not to destroy the faith essential to self-respect. Emile Zola once complained of the unjust bitterness with which his contemporaries assailed him when they were supposed to be criticising his work. In his soreness and bewilderment he asked one of the leading French men of letters what the explanation could possibly be. And it is Zola himself who records the answer which he received. It was this: "You have one immense defect which will close every door against you. You cannot chat for two minutes with an imbecile without making him feel that he is an imbecile." [*Thérèse Raquin:* Preface to French edition.] There is a difference between deflating a man's self-sufficiency and shattering a person's self-respect. Jesus ever observed that distinction. He applied the prophetic words to his own work: "A bruised reed shall he not break, and smoking flax shall he not quench, till he send forth judgment unto victory." [5] Unless we can cup our encouraging hands around the smoking flax of a sinful man's self-respect until his flickering hope flames again, we do not send judgment forth to victory, but rather to ultimate defeat.

We are saved by grace. It is also true "we are saved by hope." [6]

[3] Romans 7:24.
[4] *Ibid.*, 5:20.
[5] Matthew 12:20.
[6] Romans 8:24.

In the children of the market place calling the tunes, we see symbolized the two great traditions of the western world: the Greek and the Hebrew. The former desires fulness of life, aesthetic enjoyment, freedom from restraint. The Hebrew tradition, on the other hand, stresses righteousness, cultivates the ascetic, promotes Puritanism. As Nels Ferré puts it "The full Christian fellowship must combine the two: it can and it must find a holy happiness. . . . Liberal evangelicalism may provide the needed synthesis of these two fundamental tendencies." [7]

3. Judgment and Mercy

The gospel for the children of wisdom must make certain corrective combinations. We mention first the union of *judgment* and *mercy*. Like John on Patmos our vision should be that of the "rainbow round about the throne," the symbol of God's law and justice upholding his mercy and grace. Justice is the foundation on which every other virtue rests. "A God all mercy is a God unjust." [8] In thinking of God we must remember that his justice is fundamental to his love; and in charting our ethics we must place justice before charity or mercy.

The decent and self-respecting person says: "I want justice and not charity." The fact is that we cannot give genuine charity or mercy without first according justice. As Ruskin suggested, charity is the temple of which justice is the foundation, but we cannot have the top without the bottom. Charity comes as a result of justice. We can try to do justice to a person whether we love him or not, and our efforts at justice predispose us to good will. But if we do injustice to our brother, we come to hate him.

[7] Nels Ferré: *The Christian Fellowship*, Harper, p. 126.
[8] Edward Young: *Night Thoughts*, line 233.

In our human relations the primacy of justice is apparent. Consider the intimate love between man and woman. At marriage husband and wife may feel themselves so much in love that the questions about just and equitable arrangement of duties and money seem superfluous. But their love is not likely to remain on that high level unless it is founded on fairness and equity to both. For this reason, what is called "free love," that is, the attachment of man and woman outside the bond of matrimony, while it seems so spontaneous at the start, is likely to end in dust and ashes. One party or the other, usually the woman, has to pay too much. The marriage bond is the steel girder of justice which holds together the house of love.

Similarly in our other social relationships, mercy or charity without justice is sentimental and weak. When a father tries to be generous without first being just, he demoralizes the character of his children. When a judge essays to dispense mercy without justice, he plays havoc with law and order. When an employer substitutes a paternalistic, personal, and perhaps spasmodic, kindness for justice in his relations with his employees, he is a social liability. When philanthropy divorces charity from justice, it demoralizes the recipients of its bounty without remedying the causes of the distress. Some years ago Edith Wharton deftly depicted a woman who had a veritable passion for uplift, giving herself to all sorts of seemingly good works. But she gave no study to what justice demanded. The result was that she succeeded in upsetting rather than in uplifting. In interracial relations men often allow their personal intimacy with individual members of other races to solace their consciences while they support conventions or laws which do rank injustice to those races. Yes, justice must undergird our other virtues. "Truth is the handmaid of justice, freedom is its child, peace is its companion, safety walks in its steps, victory follows in its train; it is the brightest emanation from the Gospel: it is the attribute of God." [9]

And in our relation with God we, like the writer of Revelation, must see the throne of justice supporting the rainbow of his mercy. God is not a doting grandfather who smooths things over with a benevolent "tush, tush!" The originality of Christ's teaching about God lay not in proclaiming his Fatherhood but the holiness of that Fatherhood. As Principal Forsyth once reminded us, Jesus did not simply expand Joseph into God. There is a justice to be satisfied before mercy can be bestowed. There was a certain true insight behind the old legalistic theories of the Atonement. And while we cannot agree with the ancient theologians in thinking of Christ's life as a ransom paid to the devil or as a propitiation made to soften God's anger, nevertheless we should realize that the cross was not a mere spectacle of vicarious love designed to make men sorry enough to repent. The cross was a demonstration of the vicarious love necessary to satisfy the demands of justice. A sensitive person cannot forgive himself, nor easily accept forgiveness. The *forgiveness* of the world can only be accomplished by the *judgment* of the world.

Let us then beware of any sentimental view of justice, either human or divine. We are altogether too prone to let ourselves off and down, instead of holding ourselves up to the strict requirements of stern reality.

And now let us look at the other prong of this two-fold truth. Not only must we see the throne which supports the rainbow, we must also behold the rainbow which is round about the throne. That is, we must see the *mercy* which belongs to divine justice.

[9] Lady S. Holland: *Memoir of Sydney Smith*, Vol. I, p. 29.

What is justice? Oliver Goldsmith defined it as "the virtue which impels us to give to every person what is his due." In this he was paraphrasing Aristotle's statement, "Justice is a virtue of the soul distributing that which each person deserves." Justice is symbolized on court houses and elsewhere by the figure of a blindfolded woman with scales in her hand, the implication being that the essence of justice is the weighing of the facts in hand with an impartiality which might be lost if we could see the parties involved. But such a portrayal is hardly adequate. To put it graphically though crudely, the blindfold should be removed and spectacles should be substituted. If we would weigh a situation justly, we must see not only the persons involved, but also their backgrounds.

And when we do look into the backgrounds of persons, we see how they are caught in a meshwork of influences. We have all done wrong, run up debts and trespassed on others. And we have all been wronged, hold bad debts and been trespassed against. The sin I committed yesterday is not kept separate. It is not even like a thread woven into a piece of cloth which can be pulled out as defective; our sins flow together as waters mingle in a stream, and I can no more segregate the consequences of my sin than I can go down to Memphis and take from the Mississippi the water which flowed in from the Ohio River. I may be the most careful driver on the highway and yet be killed through the recklessness of other drivers.

Hence when we essay to do justice to others, we must make allowance for this interplay of human relations. We must try to interpret the motives behind the deeds of men, try to understand the peculiar factors of each person's personal equation. All this requires a sensitized imagination. "An imaginative man recognizes at once a portion of himself in his fellow man and speaks to that. To hurt you is to hurt himself. Much of the rudeness we encounter in life cannot be properly set down to cruelty or badness of heart. The imaginative man is sensitive and merciful to others out of the merest mercy to himself." [10] And at this point of sensitizing the imagination, religion should make a major contribution to social justice. The social imagination is not sensitized by sudden shock but by repeated exercise. And when Sunday after Sunday a congregation prays to the God and Father of all mankind its imagination should be sharpened to see how life looks to the man in Ethiopia or along the Burma Road, in Berlin or Coventry.

That imagination which enables us to see what is justly due to another is pretty close to the quality of mercy. Mercy is not a sentimental forgiveness, not a condescending pity. It is an integral part of true justice. "Justice is truth in action." [11] It is that insight which sees how life looks in the other person's place plus that kindness which gives the benefit of doubt and the days of grace to our debtors. On one occasion Andrew Bonar and Robert McCheyne, the Scottish divines, were discussing their work. McCheyne asked Bonar what his theme had been the preceding Sunday. Bonar replied, "The wicked shall be turned into hell." Quickly McCheyne came back with the question, "Were you able to preach it with tenderness?"

When we realize how we are all implicated in the social sinfulness which is now reaping the whirlwind of world calamities, we feel a sense of moral helplessness, a defence-lessness in the presence of divine judgment. This religious impotence can come pretty close to the secular feeling of

[10] Alexander Smith: *On the Importance of Man to Himself*, Oxford Press, p. 163.
[11] Benjamin Disraeli's Speech, February 11, 1851.

futility. But here the Christian faith has a message of *divine grace* and *mercy* which are combined with judgment and can re-create and empower us. The divine judgment is searching, yet as Jesus interpreted it and revealed it, it is not withering but awakening, not annihilating but creative. God in his wisdom comprehends all the factors that fashion our conduct and makes full allowance for our shortcomings. His punishments are purposive not punitive. They are purgative and not endless. His compassion is infinite. "The mercy of the Lord is from everlasting to everlasting upon them that fear him." [12]

Such is the divine justice which we are to declare in this our day of judgment. There is a "rainbow round about the throne." God rules from a "throne of grace." That old-fashioned expression has fallen into disuse. I commend it to you along with the exhortation which also may sound archaic: "Let us therefore come boldly unto the throne of grace, that we may obtain mercy and find grace to help in time of need." [13]

4. *Realism and Hope*

A second combination we need as a corrective for the children of the market place is the union of realism with hope. One characteristic of Christianity has been its invincible optimism, what Paul calls "the joy and peace of believing."

Yet while Christianity possesses a saving optimism, optimism is not always Christian. Some of us find it difficult to detect the Christlike note in an eminent premillennialist's testimony during the dark war days of 1917. The author's name is purposely withheld. He wrote: "As awful as con-

[12] Psalm 102:17.
[13] Hebrews 4:16.

ditions are across the water today, and as awful as they may become in our own country, the darker the night gets, the lighter my heart gets." The ground for such optimism was the belief that the world's darkness betokens Christ's coming in judgment to save the elect. It is hard for me to reconcile either such premillennial cheerfulness or the Barthian pessimism with the commission recorded of Jesus: "The Spirit of the Lord is upon me because he hath anointed me to preach the gospel to the poor; he hath sent me to heal the broken-hearted, to preach deliverance to the captives, and recovering of sight to the blind, to set at liberty them that are bruised, to preach the acceptable year of the Lord." [14]

Back in the 1920's it would have been well to warn the buoyant Utopianists of a *judgment* to come. It would seem equally important today to warn the Barthians of a *redemption* to come. Can we preach Christ without preaching good tidings? We have already indicated in a previous lecture why we cannot relegate Christ's redeeming grace to a realm beyond history. Can we then preach the gospel of the Kingdom if we are paralyzed by pessimism? No, we are saved by hope. But how can we be hopeful and yet realistic?

It is not enough to shout the old shibboleths of confidence. Whistling in the dark may keep up our courage for a time, but it will lag unless the light breaks. John Hampden stood as a bulwark of liberty in the struggle against autocracy. At his funeral, the service contained the Ninetieth Psalm with its great declaration: "Lord, thou hast been our dwelling-place in all generations." But on the way back from the burial, the soldiers are said to have made the valley ring with the singing of the Forty-third Psalm which

[14] Luke 4:18.

contains the prayer: "O Lord, send out thy light and thy truth, let them lead me; let them bring me unto thy holy hill." So today when the bulwarks of liberty are falling, it strengthens us to assert our faith in the Eternal; the mere repetition of such assertions has a cumulative force. But to avoid unreality we must pray for the leading of God's light and truth to bring us unto the hills whence cometh our strength.

For one thing we need to be led where we can see the *Invisibles*. I have lived long enough to know that I never see all the factors in any situation. I have walked through gardens with members of garden clubs. They have seen subtle distinctions of species and niceties of cultivation which I missed entirely. Those items were visible to them and invisible to me. I have visited art museums with artists, and while I paused to look at the pictures which I liked, they stopped before the canvases that were worth liking. They noted depths of perspective and nuances of meaning which escaped my eye. And I have to confess that I have sat in religious meetings where persons beside me were moved to depths of emotion, which I did not feel. For them God was in that place, but he was invisible to me.

I realize that around me are realms of beauty and harmony and mystic emotion which I miss. And in these dark days I am conscious that I live too much in an atmosphere of low visibility. My thoughts run in a rut of recurring ideas—wars, ruined cities and bombed homes. I need to be led out to see the worlds of the gardeners and the poets, the worlds of the artists and the saints—not that I would close my eyes to the stark realities, but that I may see life in its wholeness.

We preachers would betray our trust if we tried to give people a dainty dreamy view of our dire world. Let us look the darkest facts in the face, but let us try to see all the facts. Let us try to behold our world with the mind of Christ, remembering that Jesus was no soft emotionalist, no blind dreamer. Our Lord saw life more realistically than any other, for he viewed it from the cross. He felt the sins of the world with the sensitivity of a Savior. He did not cry "peace, peace" when there was no peace. He did not throw a halo of sentimentality around things that were hellish. But he did see life steadily and he saw it whole. As Millet said, "The end of the day is the proof of the picture." When the light is too dim for details, then the essentials must meet the test. In the twilight of our time the Christian essentials come to men. They are invisible to the worldly eye, but they are real to those who look on the things that are unseen and eternal. And in them is hope.

For another thing, we need to be led to see what Isaiah called the *treasures of darkness*. By that he meant the hidden wealth of the Israelites which would be turned over to Cyrus when he delivered Israel from bondage. As a deliverer Cyrus was a disappointment. Deeper insight was to discover the need of a deliverance more spiritual than that of the Persian King. But when Christ, the deliverer of the spirit, is come, the "treasures of darkness" are revealed. This is not the obvious comment that the night brings out the stars. Such a basis for hope is a bit too simple in our time, for while our nights bring out the stars they also bring out the bombs. We must go more deeply to uncover the "treasures of darkness."

For instance, there are the deeper insights which enrich life. The Arabs have a saying, "All sunshine makes a desert." It is so in the climate of the spirit. If we are always bland, always confident, always optimistic, our spirits grow arid, our springs of understanding dry up. Yet darkness of itself does not deepen our insights. Sorrow may becloud rather than clear our minds. Trouble may humiliate rather than humble us. Old age may sour us rather than sweeten us. May I quote these lines from my son:

> 'Tis true, old age is kinder to the soul
> Than to the body's dim, unsubtle eye,
> And slower steps seen nearer to the goal,
> But glory glances at us as we die
> And visions burn from being overbright
> As lightning kills, and passes from the sight.

Yet these deeper insights are not inevitable. Men must be guided to them. But how real and rich are the "treasures of darkness" which we ministers can help to uncover for our people! Ours is the joy of leading men into the secret of His pavilion where He hides them from the pride of man and the strife of tongues; where they feel rich in those things which moth and rust do not consume; where they prize character rather than reputation. Ours is the privilege of taking the trouble-bound mind and opening the horizon to the perspective which restores the soul. A Rhode Island friend recently paid a dubious tribute to his state. He said, "Rhode Island is a big state at low tide." So are the little patches of memory on which many are dwelling today. They look big at low tide, and our spirits have been at low ebb for some time. Our work is the divine enlargement of little memories, the penetrating of the immediate darkness with the light from the days before yesterday. This is not wishful thinking, but the corrective of wilful thinking.

And ours is the high function of strengthening souls against the depletion which may come in the days after tomorrow. It has been said that a man has only as much religion as he can command in an emergency. Ours is the privilege of helping men to be spiritually equal to emergencies, so that they can come through more than conquerors, to build their experiences into a unity like that of a ship, many parts of which would sink if separated but built together keep afloat through storm and stress. To have these deep resources is to possess the "treasures of darkness." Of these we are custodians as "stewards of God's secret truths."

Moreover, the divine light and truth can bring us unto the holy hill whence we can see the *Imponderables*. Even the most realistic recognize that every situation contains factors which cannot be measured. We can compute quite exactly the tensile strength of a bar of iron but we cannot measure with exactitude the lifting power of the person who uses it. Human strength is an imponderable and human equations cannot be computed in multiplication tables.

Human influence is another imponderable. When the grateful woman anointed our Lord's head and feet with the precious ointment, the disciples complained, "Why this waste? This might have been sold and given to the poor." [15] But Jesus answered, "Wheresoever this gospel shall be preached throughout the whole world this also that she hath done shall be spoken of as a memorial of her." It was as if Jesus were looking down the centuries and foreseeing the effect of the woman's generous deed as it would be told and retold through the years. Can anyone estimate how many icicled natures have been thawed by her act of love? Human influence is an imponderable.

And there are imponderables to be considered in our contemporary world situation, dark as it is. When Hitler marched into Paris in the summer of 1940, the *New York Times* had an editorial containing these lines: "It is only

[15] Mark 14:4-5.

the lovely shell that Hitler has captured. He has not captured the true Paris. Never can he, his tanks, his robot battalions penetrate within the walls of that magic city—Paris, where democracy had its modern rebirth: Paris that taught the world to paint and to build . . . Paris of museums, libraries, universities in which the mind could range at will: Paris the city of light . . . this is not Hitler's Paris, not today, not ever." Yes, there are immeasurable values back of the Louvre, back of the Sorbonne, back of Notre Dame. What these spiritual forces may mean for tomorrow, no man can measure.

And there are still other imponderables. Hunger haunts the overrun lands and hunger generates forces which even the Gestapo cannot control. Kindness which crosses boundaries to feed hungry peoples may make impressions which dictators cannot suppress. Seeds are harder to see than ruins and our eyes have been on the ruins; but seeds determine culture and cultures cannot be changed by a blitzkrieg. Such are some of the imponderables in our situation. From a sick room to a sick world there are factors no man can measure or predict, and realism requires that we make allowance for these. On these Jesus counted as among God's means for making foolish the wisdom of this world. We are the preachers of the Imponderables, chief of which is Christ crucified, "unto the Jews a stumblingblock, and unto the Greeks foolishness, but unto them which are called both Jews and Greeks, Christ the power of God and the wisdom of God." [16]

And along with the Invisibles, the Treasures of Darkness, the Imponderables, God's light and truth can lead us to see the Invincibles. The popular estimate of invincibles has had to be revised in recent months. Two years ago the

[16] I Corinthians 1:23-24.

French thought the Maginot Line was invincible. We know now it was not. For years the English have confidently assumed that the British Navy is invincible. We are not sure. In the exuberance of recent expansion, no doubt the Germans learned to think that Hitler's legions were invincible. Only tomorrow will tell. But tomorrow will tell that neither forts nor fleets nor armies are unconquerable. Eventually they all meet their match and are outmoded.

What then is invincible? It seems trite in this presence to mention life's three ultimates, truth, beauty and goodness. But to play on those notes, with variations of course, is the theme which makes ours "the *everlasting* gospel." And "those who know it best seem hungering and thirsting to hear it like the rest." "Truth, beauty and goodness are but different faces of the same All." [17] Truth crushed to earth will rise again. The great universities of Europe have withstood the swirling revolutions of the past; and though their buildings may be bombed, the ideals of truth for which they stand will go on. Beauty will survive the uglification of scarring wars. James Hilton a few years ago grew so fearful that our battling western nations would destroy their works of art that he pictured his fanciful *Shangri-la* where time and wars left no mark. But in another book Hilton himself created a character called "Mr. Chips" whose beauty of character blossomed right through the World War. Beauty survives brutality. Artists will paint tomorrow. Poets will sing tomorrow. "Beauty seen is never lost." [18] And as for goodness, it does seem that about everything the world's Best Man stood for is being challenged. But the Black Friday on which he was crucified

[17] Ralph Waldo Emerson: *Essay on Nature.*
[18] John Greenleaf Whittier: "Sunset on the Bearcamp."

became the Good Friday of history, because the character revealed on the cross vindicates its rightness in the hearts of men down the ages.

When my former teacher, the distinguished historian, Charles A. Beard, was asked what lessons he had learned from his lifelong study and teaching of history, he struck off these lines:

1. The mills of the gods grind slowly but they grind exceeding fine;
2. Those whom the gods are about to destroy they first make mad;
3. When it gets dark enough, you can see stars;
4. The bee fertilizes the flower that it robs.[19]

These convictions, distilled from a long and rich experience, serve as steps by which realism rises to hope. The slow but inevitable working of divine justice; the suicidal futility of anger; the fertilization of life through sacrifice are lessons which give confidence when the darkness becomes deepest.

[19] Personal letter to the author dated May 12, 1941.

THE LYMAN BEECHER LECTURES ON PREACHING [1]

Yale University Divinity School

Established May 2, 1872 by Mr. Henry W. Sage in honor of Reverend Lyman Beecher, D.D.

1871–1872   Henry Ward Beecher, *Yale Lectures on Preaching*, first series, N.Y., J. B. Ford & Company, 1872.

1872–1873   Henry Ward Beecher, *Yale Lectures on Preaching*, second series, N.Y., J. B. Ford & Company, 1873.

1873–1874   Henry Ward Beecher, *Yale Lectures on Preaching*, third series, N.Y., J. B. Ford & Company, 1874. A one volume edition, *Yale Lectures on Preaching*, published by The Pilgrim Press, Chicago.

1874–1875   John Hall, *God's Word Through Preaching*. N.Y., Dodd & Mead, 1875.

1875–1876   William Mackergo Taylor, *The Ministry of the Word*. N.Y., Anson D. F. Randolph & Co., 1876.

1876–1877   Phillips Brooks, *Lectures on Preaching*. N.Y., E. P. Dutton, 1877.

1877–1878   Robert William Dale, *Nine Lectures on Preaching*. N.Y., A. S. Barnes & Co., 1878.

1878–1879   Matthew Simpson, *Lectures on Preaching*. N.Y., Nelson & Phillips, 1879.

1879–1880   Howard Crosby, *The Christian Preacher*. N.Y., Anson D. F. Randolph & Co., 1880.

[1] Compiled by Reverend Hal Earl Norton, D.D., Pastor, The Roundy Memorial Baptist Church, Milwaukee, Wisconsin.

1880–1881   Joseph Tuthill Duryea, George Harris, Samuel E. Herrick, Nathaniel Judson Burton, and Llewelyn David Bevan. Lectures not published.

1881–1882   Ezekiel Gilman Robinson, *Lectures on Preaching*. N.Y., Henry Holt & Company, Inc., 1883.

1882–1883   No lectures.

1883–1884   Nathaniel Judson Burton, *Yale Lectures on Preaching and Other Writings*. Pilgrim Press, 1887. Reprinted by Macmillan Company, 1925, under title of *In Pulpit and Parish*.

1884–1885   Henry Martin Storrs, *The American Preacher*. Not published.

1885–1886   William Mackergo Taylor, *The Scottish Pulpit*. N.Y., Harper & Brothers, 1887.

1886–1887   Washington Gladden, *Tools and the Man*. Boston, Houghton Mifflin Company, 1893.

1887–1888   Henry Clay Trumbull, *The Sunday School*. Philadelphia, John P. Wattles, 1888.

1888–1889   John Albert Broadus, *Preparation and Delivery of Sermons*. N.Y., Harper & Brothers, 1897.

1889–1890   Adolphus Julius Frederick Behrends, *The Philosophy of Preaching*. N.Y., Charles Scribner's Sons, 1893.

1890–1891   James Stalker, *The Preacher and His Models*. N.Y., A. C. Armstrong, 1893.

1891–1892   Andrew Martin Fairbairn, *The Place of Christ in Modern Theology*. N.Y., Charles Scribner's Sons, 1893.

1892–1893   Robert Foreman Horton, *Verbum Dei*. N.Y., Macmillan Company, 1893.

1893–1894   No lectures.

1894–1895   David Hummell Greer, *The Preacher and His Place*. N.Y., Charles Scribner's Sons, 1895.

1895–1896   Henry van Dyke, *The Gospel for an Age of Doubt*. N.Y., Macmillan Company, 1896

1896–1897   John Watson (Ian Maclaren), *The Cure of Souls.* N.Y., Dodd & Mead, 1896.

1897–1898   William Jewett Tucker, *The Making and the Unmaking of the Preacher.* Boston, Houghton Mifflin Company, 1898.

1898–1899   Sir George Adam Smith, *Modern Criticism and the Preaching of the Old Testament.* N.Y., A. C. Armstrong, 1901.

1899–1900   John Brown, *Puritan Preaching in England.* N.Y., Charles Scribner's Sons, 1900.

1900–1901   No lectures.

1901–1902   Washington Gladden, *Social Salvation.* Boston, Houghton Mifflin Company, 1902.

1902–1903   George Angier Gordon, *Ultimate Conceptions of Faith.* Boston, Houghton Mifflin Company, 1903.

1903–1904   Lyman Abbott, *The Christian Ministry.* Boston, Houghton Mifflin Company, 1905.

1904–1905   Francis Greenwood Peabody, *Jesus Christ and the Christian Character.* N.Y., Macmillan Company, 1908.

1905–1906   Charles Reynolds Brown, *The Social Message of the Modern Pulpit.* N.Y., Charles Scribner's Sons, 1906.

1906–1907   Peter Taylor Forsyth, *Positive Preaching and the Modern Mind.* London, Hodder & Stoughton, 1907.

1907–1908   William Herbert Perry Faunce, *The Educational Ideal in the Ministry.* N.Y., Macmillan Company, 1908; reprinted 1919.

1908–1909   Herbert Hensley Hensen, *The Liberty of Prophesying.* New Haven, Yale University Press, 1910.

1909–1910   Charles Edward Jefferson, *The Building of the Church.* N.Y., Macmillan Company, 1910.

1910–1911   Frank Wakeley Gunsaulus, *The Minister and the Spiritual Life.* N.Y., Fleming H. Revell, 1911.

1911–1912   John Henry Jowett, *The Preacher: His Life and Work*. N.Y., George H. Doran, 1912.

1912–1913   Charles Henry Parkhurst, *The Pulpit and the Pew*. New Haven, Yale University Press, 1913.

1913–1914   Charles Sylvester Horne, *The Romance of Preaching*. N.Y., Fleming H. Revell, 1914.

1914–1915   George Wharton Pepper, *A Voice from the Crowd*. New Haven, Yale University Press, 1915.

1915–1916   William DeWitt Hyde, *The Gospel of Good Will*. N.Y., Macmillan Company, 1916.

1916–1917   William Fraser McDowell, *Good Ministers of Jesus Christ*. N.Y., Abingdon Press, 1917.

1917–1918   Henry Sloane Coffin, *In a Day of Social Rebuilding*. New Haven, Yale University Press, 1918.

1918–1919   John Kelman, *The War and Preaching*. New Haven, Yale University Press, 1919.

1919–1920   Albert Parker Fitch, *Preaching and Paganism*. New Haven, Yale University Press, 1920.

1920–1921   Charles David Williams, *The Prophetic Ministry for Today*. N.Y., Macmillan Company, 1921.

1921–1922   William Pierson Merrill, *The Freedom of the Preacher*. N.Y., Macmillan Company, 1922.

1922–1923   Charles Reynolds Brown, *The Art of Preaching*. N.Y., Macmillan Company, 1922.

1923–1924   Harry Emerson Fosdick, *The Modern Use of the Bible*. N.Y., Macmillan Company, 1924.

1924–1925   William Ralph Inge, *The Preaching of the Kingdom of God in History*. Lectures not published.

1925–1926   Raymond Calkins, *The Eloquence of the Christian Experience*. N.Y., Macmillan Company, 1927.

1926–1927   John Robert Paterson Sclater, *The Public Worship of God*. N.Y., Doubleday, Doran, 1927.

1927–1928   James Edward Freeman, *The Ambassador*. N.Y., Macmillan Company, 1928.

1928–1929   Edwin Du Bose Mouzon, *Preaching with Authority*. N.Y., Macmillan Company, 1929.

1929–1930   Francis John McConnell, *The Prophetic Ministry*. N.Y., Abingdon Press, 1930.

1930–1931   George Arthur Buttrick, *Jesus Came Preaching*. N.Y., Charles Scribner's Sons, 1931.

1931–1932   Ernest Fremont Tittle, *Jesus After Nineteen Centuries*. N.Y., Abingdon Press, 1932.

1932–1933   Lawrence Pearsall Jacks, *Elemental Religion*. N.Y., Harper & Brothers, 1934.

1933–1934   Albert Edward Day, *Jesus and Human Personality*. N.Y., Abingdon Press, 1934.

1934–1935   Walter Russell Bowie, *The Renewing Gospel*. N.Y., Charles Scribner's Sons, 1935.

1935–1936   John Edgar Park, *The Miracle of Preaching*. N.Y., Macmillan Company, 1936.

1936–1937   No lectures.

1937–1938   Willard Learoyd Sperry, *We Prophesy in Part*. N.Y., Harper & Brothers, 1938.

1938–1939   Charles Clayton Morrison, *What Is Christianity?* Chicago, Willett, Clark & Company, 1940.

1939–1940   George Arthur Buttrick, Edwin McNeill Poteat, Arthur Howe Bradford, Elmore McNeill McKee, Wyatt Aiken Smart, and Ernest Fremont Tittle, *Preaching in These Times*. N.Y., Charles Scribner's Sons, 1940.

1940–1941   Ralph Washington Sockman, *The Highway of God*. N.Y., Macmillan Company, 1942.

INDEX

" Half cured Souls " see Page 146-7